a green guide to
bringing up your baby

a green guide to
bringing up your baby

the kind way for you, your baby (0–3)
and the environment

claire gillman

CICO BOOKS
LONDON NEW YORK

This book is dedicated to our very dear and much-loved friend, Britta Faulkner (04.08.64 – 08.08.08), who was a wonderfully loving and natural mother.

Published in 2009 by **CICO Books**
an imprint of Ryland Peters & Small Ltd
20–21 Jockey's Fields, London WC1R 4BW

www.cicobooks.co.uk

10 9 8 7 6 5 4 3 2 1

A CIP catalogue record for this book is available from the British Library.

ISBN 978 1906525 86 6

Printed in Hong Kong

Editor: Marion Paull
Designer: Barbara Zuñiga
Illustrator: Trina Dalziel
For photography credits, please see page 160.

Please note that the advice in this book is not to be considered as a substitute for medical advice from your family doctor or any other qualified medical practitioner. If you treat your child with natural medicines, such as herbs, you should always inform your doctor, because these can be very powerful and can interact with prescribed and over-the-counter medications.

Contents

Introduction   6

Chapter 1: Nurture and Care   8
Bonding   10
Early Feeding Options   14
Weaning   20
Teething   23
Early Foods   27
Sleep   34

**Chapter 2: Healthy Home
  Environment   40**
Nursery Ecology   42
Natural Baby Equipment   49
Keeping House   52
Pollutants   57
Clothing and Baby Toiletries   63

Chapter 3: Natural Learning   66
Creating a Positive
  Learning Environment   68
Early Childcare Provisions   72
Home Schooling   78
Emotional Intelligence   81
Body Language   87

Chapter 4: Play and Creativity   90
Dance, Music and Movement   92
Creative Play   96
Imaginary Play   100
Storytelling   104
Creative Art   108
Energy Burning   110

Chapter 5: Health and Healing 112
Baby Health   114
  Colic   114
  Nappy Rash   117
  Cradle Cap   118
Common Complaints   121
  Diarrhoea   121
  Ear Infection   123
  Fever   124
The Immune System   126
  Coughs and Colds   126
  Chicken Pox   128
  Mumps   129
The Great Outdoors   130
  Insect Bites   130
  First Aid   132
  Motion Sickness   135

Chapter 6: Natural Therapies 136
Acupressure   138
Chiropractic   140
Massage   142
Osteopathy   146
Homeopathy   148
Medical Herbalism   150

Milestones   152
Useful Contacts   156
Index   158
**Acknowledgements
  and Picture Credits   160**

Introduction

Becoming a parent is probably the biggest life change you will ever experience and, it seems to me, a wonderful opportunity to re-evaluate the way you live your life. If you are not already an active and ardent eco-enthusiast, now is the perfect time to start embracing a more natural way of life.

A greener approach will not only benefit your new baby by providing her with the healthiest and most natural environment in which to grow and thrive, but it will also promote a healthier future for you and your whole family and, as an additional and welcome bonus, benefit our planet, too.

So the aim of this book is to help you to bring up your baby in the most natural way possible in a manner that fits in with your particular beliefs, aims and lifestyle. Some of you will be keen to adopt the vast majority of the advice contained in these pages. Others will be happy to cherry-pick the suggestions that best resonate with you. Either way is fine. There's plenty to choose from.

In the following pages, we look at numerous areas of everyday life where you can make small changes that will introduce a greener and healthier element to your child's upbringing. These are not radical, wacky ideas but practical lifestyle modifications that anyone can adopt and that will bring far-reaching benefits. Topics range from healthy early foods through natural baby clothes and nursery ecology to the benefits of massage and other natural therapies.

In light of the fact that a decade ago virtually no organic baby food was available in the UK and today one baby in three eats organic food – the organic baby food market is growing by 50 per cent per year compared with 5 per cent for its non-organic equivalent – I think it's fair to say that today's parents are increasingly interested in a green approach to

bringing up baby. Since you are reading this, you probably count yourself among the growing band of parents who wish to act on this new awareness.

Actually, without wishing to sound a pessimistic note, your interest in green parenting could not be more opportune. Given that the number of obese children in the UK has tripled in the past twenty years and is still rising – currently one in ten six-year-olds is obese and half of all children could be obese by 2020 – starting your baby off on healthy natural foods from the outset, which is known to promote healthier eating habits in your child's later life, is a great investment in her future.

Similarly, the practical common-sense advice on how to protect your child from unnecessary exposure to harmful chemicals and pollutants in the home is another worthwhile insurance for your child's present and future health. It is staggering to think that the average western home contains more than 150 different kitchen and bathroom cleaning products, and the effects of this heady cocktail on infant health are not as yet fully understood. Swapping to some of the cleaning agents that our grandmothers used is not a retrograde step – these are safe, efficient and they've stood the test of time.

As your baby grows into a young child, I hope that you will revisit the chapters expounding the green approach to natural learning and creative play, and that the ideas and suggestions they contain will excite and entice you towards creating a learning environment that responds to and supports your child's natural learning endeavours.

The two final chapters are devoted to natural health and healing for common childhood ailments and an exploration of the natural therapies that you might consider adopting for any health problems, yours or your child's.

Although our modern lives in general are physically easier than those of our forebears, emotionally I don't think there has ever been a harder time to raise a family. Parents are under enormous pressure to get it right, to produce high-achieving, educationally successful children. Sad to say, both

parents and children are judged by these yardsticks rather than by whether or not you have raised children who are happy, calm, healthy individuals. Worse still, there is so much conflicting and confusing advice in the media for new parents, it's hard to know what to believe and how to sift the hype from the facts. As a general rule of thumb, I think that parents instinctively know what is right for their child and for their family and, as a starting point, you should trust your intuition.

If you feel drawn to a green lifestyle and you want a more natural, healthier up-bringing for your child, the information contained in this book covers much of what you're looking for. It is by no means exhaustive but there should be more than enough in the way of practical suggestions here to set you on the path to a greener way to raise your baby.

Nurture & Care

As new parents, you are likely to be painfully conscious of your responsibilities as protectors and providers for your baby. You are fastidious about meeting all her physical needs and have probably gone to great lengths to provide the mountain of equipment, care and attention needed to keep your child safe and comfortable.

Yet the emotional care that you shower on your baby is just as important as her physical well-being. Your loving, tender response to your baby (see Bonding, page 10) will set the tone for her development and help to create the nurturing environment in which your child will flourish.

In this chapter, we will look at some of the most pressing questions of natural babycare for many new parents. Common dilemmas such as whether to breast- or bottle-feed (see page 14) and when/how to wean your baby (see page 20) are discussed.

As she matures from baby to toddler, you will face decisions regarding other key developmental milestones, including establishing good sleeping patterns (see page 34), getting your child to eat healthily (see page 27) and dealing with teething issues (see page 23).

Once you have made the seamless, natural transition from expectant parents to small family unit, you will probably be amazed at just how this tiny individual compels you to look after her and, just as miraculously, how delighted you are to nurture and care for her in your own unique way.

Bonding

As your little scrap of scrunched up humanity is placed in your arms for the first time, you may well be bombarded by a baffling array of emotions. Most parents expect to feel love at first sight and, for the lucky few, this happens. However, for many new parents, love is not instantaneous.

A new mother is more likely to experience a feeling of bewilderment, often relief that the pain and exertion are over, perhaps a kind of wonderment but, most commonly, new mothers report a sort of numbness when first presented with their newborns.

Given that these reactions are commonplace, the romantic notion that blood ties, hormones or even the process of giving birth itself will miraculously cause a woman to bond with her baby is thoroughly unrealistic. It is this high expectation of instantaneous love that causes many new mothers to feel guilty or ashamed of their apparent lack of feelings, but you mustn't.

It is perfectly normal to bond gradually over the first few weeks or months of your baby's life and this gentle approach can be hugely rewarding. As long as you attend to your baby's needs sensitively and are attentive and caring, the baby will not suffer if it's not love at first sight. In the great scheme of things, a few weeks here or there really don't matter in a lifetime of loving. As long as you love him later, no harm will be done.

Forming Bonds

For most parents, the urge to cuddle and protect, if not love, their baby is very strong. In the early days, your baby's helplessness and utter dependence on you is often enough for a loving bond to develop. It is this bond that gets you up in the middle of the night despite your exhaustion and helps you to respond to his cries.

For some, this early dependence is too demanding or too much of a one-way deal and it is not until the relationship is more reciprocal that the bond develops. The first smile or some other indication of

From a very early age, your baby will try to imitate your facial expressions and he can follow moving objects with his eyes. These are all tools for forming a loving attachment between you.

responsiveness is often a turning point, particularly for new fathers.

The good news for human survival is that, irrespective of your feelings, a baby will instinctively seek out someone to protect him. From birth, a baby will cling, cuddle, make eye contact and respond to an adult's efforts to soothe him – all responses designed to stimulate our bonding instincts.

Often the bonding process takes place unnoticed as you go about the daily routine of caring for your baby and it's not until he smiles at you and you're engulfed by feelings of love and joy that you realize bonding has occurred naturally.

Some parents enjoy an intense attachment to their baby in the first few minutes, hours or days but for everyone else, bonding is a process of adaptation that brings with it huge rewards and pleasures. If key people in the baby's life, such as grandparents, want to bond successfully, it's important for them to be involved with the care of the baby as soon as possible. Bathing him, bottle-feeding where applicable, or simply cuddling and talking to him all aid the bonding procedure. Remember, there's no one right way of dealing with a baby but the aim is always the same – to build a loving and trusting relationship.

Delayed Bonding

In some instances, there are more tangible reasons for delayed bonding. If you've had a particularly traumatic birth, you're depressed, your baby is in an incubator or needs special care, or if he is handicapped, you may feel alienated, impotent and distant from him.

Similarly, if you have your heart set specifically on a boy or a girl and deliver the opposite sex, this can cause problems in early bonding. Fixed expectations that are not met often impede the bonding process. This early rejection does not often last long and usually reverts very quickly to overwhelming feelings of protection and eventually love.

greenfile

A great way to aid bonding is to give your baby a massage regularly, which is relaxing and pleasurable for you both. For further details on infant massage, see page 142.

WARNING It's common for women to feel ambivalent about the baby but if you or your family and friends feel that this is not simply a case of 'baby blues' and that you may have post-natal depression, or you wish your baby harm, you should speak to your GP or health visitor without delay.

However, it is important to recognize these feelings and, if possible, give voice to them. The need to talk about labour and delivery is strong in all mothers. However, if you've been horrified to discover that not only do you not instantly love your baby but that you don't even want anything to do with him, you may feel ashamed and less inclined to speak. If you silently bottle up your feelings of guilt, you will find it increasingly difficult to work through the problems of the birth and your reaction, and this will delay your chances of bonding still further. Talk to your midwife or health visitor about your feelings as well as to your partner and friends.

Whatever your experience of the bonding process, the most important thing to remember is that the bond almost invariably develops between you sooner or later but it is less likely to grow if you are tense, depressed or feeling guilty about your initial reactions. The more you worry about not falling in love with your baby, the harder it is to achieve.

helping the bonding process

Dismiss ideas that bonding should be instant or exclusively for mothers and don't allow yourself to feel guilty if there's not an immediate bond.

Make sure that you and your partner have undistracted time together with the baby.

Make your baby feel loved by talking or singing to him and providing cuddles and stimulation but remember to give him time to rest and relax.

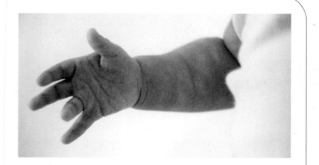

Take the opportunity to be 'skin to skin' with your newborn by holding him against your own skin when feeding or cradling or sharing a bath with him.

Make eye-to-eye contact at close range because this helps meaningful communication.

As long as you and the baby are well, keep hospital stays to a minimum – being treated like a visitor can undermine a new father's confidence.

Get plenty of rest, relaxation and eat healthy food.

Plan for paternity leave (or its alternative) – ideally two weeks – to start when you get home. This should be a time for celebration and for the new family unit to get to know one another. Make sure you are both involved in the care of the baby.

Don't overwhelm your baby, talk at him or be over-intrusive. Rather, take your cues from him and be emotionally responsive.

If you experience high anxiety and/or feel exhausted and isolated, make sure you get some practical support and plenty of reassurance.

Don't put yourself under unnecessary pressure by expecting everything to be perfect.

Many new mums report feelings of social isolation that can cause resentment against their baby and impair the bonding experience. Make sure you meet others in similar situations by joining mother and toddler groups or contacting the National Childbirth Trust (NCT), which is a charitable organization providing support and information for parents (see Useful Contacts, page 156). Establish a network of friends and ask for advice and discuss concerns.

Early Feeding Options

Although it is normally the mother who decides whether a baby is to be breast- or bottle-fed, it is often a partner's caring support that allows her to stick to that decision, particularly if she's having early difficulties with breast-feeding, for example. So, while it should be your decision, be sure you have your partner's support about that choice. If you are going to be largely on your own, trust your own judgement, but why not discuss your thoughts and reasoning with friends and professionals?

Breast milk is known to meet your baby's needs perfectly and is digested easily, but your baby won't suffer if you decide to bottle-feed. Feeding your baby should be a pleasure, not a challenge, and it won't be if you breast-feed from a sense of obligation, or bottle-feed while feeling guilty. Don't let anyone make you feel bad about your choice – it's a highly personal and very emotive issue.

However, there is one proviso. Once you've started with bottles, you can't switch to breast-feeding – without the stimulation of your baby sucking, your breasts will stop producing milk. So even if you instinctively feel you'd like to bottle-feed or you don't like the idea of breast-feeding particularly, it may still be worth putting off a final decision until the baby is born and you've given breast-feeding a try.

Also, it is scientifically proven that there is no substitute for the colostrum that your breasts produce in the first few days after the birth, and this provides the valuable antibodies essential for your baby to fight infection in the early months. So even if you breast-feed for a day or two only, it's of benefit to your baby.

Whichever method of feeding you decide upon, remember that the closeness, love, cuddling and attention that the baby receives at this special time are just as important as the milk that you give him. A relaxed feeding time will be deeply rewarding for both you and your baby. A few of the specific pros and cons peculiar to each option can be found on page 18.

Knowing the facts is one thing but trusting your instincts is also very important. Talk to friends and other new mums about their experiences and why they are happy (or otherwise) with the feeding choices they made. Seeing the feeding experience and how it works in practice for others may help you to decide what will work best for you and your lifestyle.

Lack of Sleep

Irrespective of your feeding decision, resign yourself to the fact that you will be up during the night to feed the baby for the first few months. Most mothers now feed 'on demand', which simply means whenever the baby is hungry, rather than following a timetable. There is nothing to be gained by keeping your baby waiting once he starts crying to be fed. You're not spoiling him by answering his needs – an accusation sometimes levelled by the 'old-school' of parenting.

As his digestive system matures and grows, he'll take more at each feed and the intervals between feeds will become longer, but for the first six to eight weeks, your baby can probably not go much longer than two to four hours between feeds. This is tolerable during the day but can be exhausting at night. Even if you are taking the precaution of going to bed early and cat-napping in the day, you will still not be getting more than a few hours' sleep in one stretch and this is what becomes so tiring. After a week or so, you'll feel dazed and possibly quite weepy – hardly surprising really when you think that the military use sleep deprivation to weaken the resolve of prisoners of war.

The only consolation is that you know it will come to an end, hopefully soon, and that it can only get better. But while you're going through the sleepless-night period, it's hard to hold on to that

> The size of your breasts has no relevance to their ability to produce an abundant supply of milk. Milk is produced in deeply buried glands, not in the surrounding fatty tissue of the breast.

thought, or believe it. Don't be surprised or feel guilty if you resent your beloved baby for waking you up yet again. You are not alone if you burst into tears because the baby won't settle after a night feed and you're desperate to get back to bed. You may even find yourself shooting your partner hateful looks as he appears to sleep soundly next to you. Never mind that he is also having disturbed nights or has been helping with the feeding routine – just being inert next to you is enough to make you seethe. All this is perfectly natural and being able to discuss it with girlfriends and even laugh about it can make it more bearable.

Breast-feeding

Although you may think that breast-feeding is perfectly natural and therefore it should be easy, some new mothers have genuine difficulties in mastering the technique. Midwives are excellent at offering help in the early days but if you're still struggling when their visits have ceased, why not contact your local branch of the La Leche League or the NCT, who have breast-feeding counsellors who can help you personally.

Breast-feeding is more time-consuming in the early weeks, partly because a breast-fed baby wants to feed more frequently than a bottle-fed one. One reason for that is that he likes to suck. In fact, sucking is a need and a pleasure quite distinct from the need for food.

Once you've settled into a routine with feeding and are completely relaxed about it, you'll find breast-feeding extremely convenient – it allows you the freedom to travel uncluttered, the milk is always there, always sterile and always at the temperature your baby likes. The downside, of course, is that if you're solely breast-feeding, you're tied to being close

to your baby for feed times. The way round that one is to express milk so that someone else can feed your baby – remember to make provisions for while you're out so that you can express at your normal feed time because your breasts will be full. And don't forget to take breast-pads with you – you don't want to be embarrassed by milk leaking through your smart clothes or new gladrags.

All the time you are breast-feeding, you must also take care about what you eat and drink, and any medications you might take, since minute amounts of anything ingested will pass into the milk and so affect your baby. You will soon find what adversely affects

---

greenfile

Make sure you have a glass of water next to you when you breast-feed. You need to drink a great deal for good milk production.

---

natural remedies for common breast-feeding problems

Sore and cracked nipples occur when the baby suckles the nipple instead of the whole aureola:
• Apply a tablespoon of olive oil mixed with the juice of half a lemon four times a day (but wash off before feeding) at the first hint of nipple soreness.
• Cracked nipples benefit from calendula cream.
• Nipple guards may help.

Engorged breasts result if your milk production exceeds demand, perhaps if you're overdue with a feed, for example:

• Express excess milk by hand or pump.
• Soak breasts in a hot bath or apply hot flannels or heat pads.
• Sometimes ice packs (wrapped in a flannel) may help if heat does not.
• Place cabbage leaves from the fridge or freezer inside your bra for immediate relief.

him (in my experience grapes cause chaos) but there may be times when you think, 'What the hell, I really fancy a chicken vindaloo – just this once.' It may be worth it for the pleasure, but rest assured, you'll almost certainly pay the price the next day with an unsettled, upset baby and the most disgusting nappies ever!

Bottle-feeding

For some, the freedom that bottle-feeding affords far outweighs the benefits of breast-feeding. Certainly, someone else can help with feeds, and fathers often become more involved at an earlier stage with bottle-fed babies.

Bottle-fed babies are often able to last longer between feeds because formula milk is usually digested more slowly than breast milk. This means that you will probably get longer stretches of uninterrupted sleep in the early days but (and there's always a but, isn't there!), once awake, a bottle feed takes longer due to the preparation time and having to warm the milk.

Although preparing and sterilizing bottles will almost certainly become a chore after a few weeks, it is essential that you remain fastidious in their cleaning – if your baby picks up micro-organisms from poorly cleaned bottles causing diarrhoea and vomiting, he could be very seriously ill. Also, make sure you don't use formula that has passed its expiration date, avoid dented or damaged tins and throw away milk left in the bottle or any that has been at room temperature for more than half an hour.

At least with a bottle, you know exactly how much milk your baby has taken. Try to trust his appetite. With formula milk, it's so easy to overfeed, which can lead to him being overweight.

Most infant formulas are based on cow's milk that is modified to resemble human milk, and fortified with vitamins, such as K and D, and iron. However, a few babies have difficulty with formula milk. About 2.5 per cent of infants under three may be allergic to cow's milk. Symptoms include vomiting, diarrhoea, colic, skin rashes, frequent ear infections, nasal congestion and sluggishness. For these babies, a soya-based formula is advised but you should check with your doctor first.

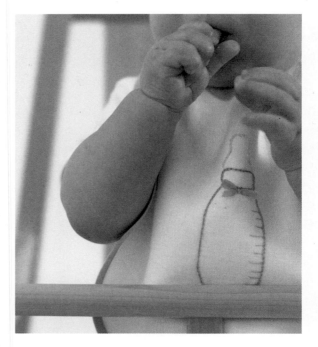

When travelling, the bottle-making palaver can be simplified by using ready-to-feed formulas from cartons or cans – you simply open and pour into the bottle. The baby can even drink it at room temperature if necessary. However, once opened, ready-to-feed formula should be covered and refrigerated.

Finally, there have been some concerns voiced about the possibility of a potentially toxic chemical in plastic, known as Bisphenol A (BPA) leaching from baby bottles. Where possible, avoid hard polycarbonate plastic, which contains BPA. Instead, use bottles made of glass, or BPA-free plastic (check the label). As an additional precaution:

• Discard worn bottles (those that are cloudy or scratched). Chemicals leach into food more easily when plastics break down.
• Don't fill bottles with boiling water.
• Don't leave plastic baby bottles in hot cars or in direct sunlight.

Don't be put off by any of the disadvantages mentioned above. There is always a downside to every decision you take and, as long as you feel confident you have made the right decision for you and your baby, none of these obstacles are insurmountable.

at-a-glance arguments for breast-feeding

• Initially, your baby will get colostrum from the breast. This will protect his health while he builds his own immune system.

• Your milk is uniquely right for your baby, especially if he arrived early (known as pre-term), and continues to be so as he grows. It also adjusts to surroundings, so if it's hot weather, your milk provides extra water for your baby.

• If your baby is genetically predisposed to allergies, breast-feeding will protect him from early exposure to 'foreign' milk proteins until his digestive system is better developed.

• Recent studies suggest that breast-feeding helps to optimize brain development and minimize the chances of neurological problems.

• Your uterus and your figure return to pre-pregnancy shape much faster.

• Once established, nursing releases hormones that help to relax you and to combat stress.

• Breast-feeding forces you to sit down and take the rest you need.

• Breast-feeding is thought to reduce the risk of breast cancer developing before the menopause.

at-a-glance arguments for bottle-feeding

• Getting a baby started on the bottle is easier than on the breast because you only have to consider his comfort and not your own.

• Using formula milk from the beginning avoids the intense and sometimes uncomfortable physical contact with your baby that breast-feeding requires.

• The bond between father and baby may be closer because he can feed the baby from the outset.

• If you are not breast-feeding, your body is no longer providing for the baby, so it can belong to you again.

• With formula, you know exactly how much milk your baby has taken.

Weaning

Weaning is one of the early milestones for both mother and baby. Giving up the breast or bottle on which your baby has depended since birth undoubtedly brings greater independence for him but, for some mothers, it can be an emotional hurdle. Here are some tips for making it easier for the whole family.

Timing

When you actually start the process and how you proceed is up to you, although health professionals recommend that you do not introduce solids before four months and preferably not before six months.

Often parents find that the initiative is taken by the baby, who starts to lose interest in feeding from the breast or bottle. For others, when the first teeth come through is a good time to start weaning.

As well as a means of providing food, breast and bottle represent comfort and safety to your baby. For that reason, make sure that you choose your time wisely to introduce weaning. If there are other major changes in his life, such as starting at a nursery or with a childminder, or if he is ill, you should put it off for a few more weeks. Similarly, if you are under stress, about to go back to work or on holiday, it's probably not a good time to attempt weaning.

Introducing Solids

When you first start weaning, you are simply introducing your baby to different tastes, textures and consistencies, and to the idea of eating from a spoon. During the first few weeks, milk will still provide him with all the nourishment that he needs.

Start by offering a few small tastes of baby rice, or fruit or vegetable purée (see right for suggestions) at one feed. Most parents opt for the lunchtime feed, which is often less fraught than breakfast. Avoid teatime because of the possibility that the newly introduced food may upset your baby, giving you both a disturbed night.

He may take to the idea better if you partially satisfy his hunger first, so 'sandwich' a teaspoon or two of purée between two halves of his normal breast- or

Initially, babies can digest yellow and orange vegetables more easily than green vegetables.

bottle-feed. Allow yourself plenty of time because this process can be time-consuming.

Finally, don't try to rush things. Eventually, you'll be able to drop one milk feed altogether, but leave at least three days before dropping another. This schedule allows your baby to adjust and, if you are breast-feeding, for your milk production to wind down. Also, introduce just one new food at a time – that way, if there is an adverse reaction, you'll be able to identify the culprit and avoid it in future.

Home-cooked or commercial baby foods?

Home-made food has an infinite variety of taste and texture, and it prepares your

greenfile

If your baby is thirsty, water is far and away the best option, although diluted fruit juice can be thirst quenching. Wherever possible, use a domestic purifier for tap-water or choose still bottled water, but check that it does not contain high levels of salt or other minerals.

baby for eating with the family when he's older. Wherever possible, choose organic fruits and vegetables for your baby's meals.

Baby foods in jars, cans and packets can be useful, especially when travelling or if you're in a hurry. When choosing commercial food, carefully check the list of ingredients and avoid any that show sugar, dextrose, sucrose, salt or water as predominating. Pre-packaged organic baby foods are readily available and are a good alternative to home-prepared foods.

Powdered baby cereals are also a boon. They are rich in vitamins, fortified with iron and use valuable additional milk (either expressed breast, formula or cow's) in the mixing.

Preparing purées

1 Peel, chop and steam whichever fruit or vegetable you're using until it's soft.

2 Blend in a liquidizer or mouli, adding some of the reserved cooking water or breast milk/formula milk to thin if necessary (you're aiming for a thick soup consistency).

3 Allow to cool before serving to your baby.

4 Any excess purée can be poured into ice-cube trays and frozen for future feeding sessions.

Popular fruit purées: apple, pear, mashed banana (no need to cook), mango, peach. Avoid kiwi fruit, citrus fruits, strawberries, and raspberries until he's over six months.
Popular vegetable purées: butternut squash, sweet potato, carrot, courgette, swede, green bean, parsnip, avocado (no need to cook).

WARNING While cow's milk is suitable for cooking, it shouldn't replace either breast or formula milk as a drink until your child is 12 months old as it lacks the iron content required by young babies.

Teething

Nature played a rather cruel trick on mankind when she arranged it so that no sooner have parents got their new arrival settled into something resembling a routine than a baby's first teeth start to appear.

For the majority of babies, teething starts in the second half of their first year, but there can be a wide range in the ages at which babies cut their first tooth. Baby teeth almost invariably come through in the same order. Generally, the lower central incisors (in the middle of the bottom jaw) come through at about six months and by her first birthday, a baby has about ten teeth. The back molars appear around the end of the second year and, by the age of two and a half, most children have all twenty of their baby teeth.

Don't be too concerned if a recent achievement drops away during the teething period. Children often regress but once the pain has subsided, your baby will soon be practising those skills again.

Teething Troubles

How much discomfort a baby experiences during this process varies from child to child but you'll be very lucky to get away with no disturbance at all. For some infants, the pain can be quite severe and they will need some form of pain relief, while others seem to experience only mild discomfort.

Even if your baby is one of the fortunate few and sails through early teething, you should expect some upset when the back molars come through at around the end of the second year. These teeth are broad and blunt and often cause more problems when they break the gum than the smaller, sharper front teeth.

Red, sore gums and a particularly flushed cheek on one side often indicate teething. You may also notice that your baby is dribbling a great deal and that she

dental care

Although tooth decay is fairly unusual in primary teeth, once it starts, the teeth deteriorate very quickly because of the high ratio of soft inner to hard enamel outer. As well as causing pain, their decay can affect the development of the permanent teeth below, so establishing good dental hygiene from the earliest age is most important.

• As soon as a couple of teeth appear, start cleaning them with a soft toothbrush and a very small amount of children's toothpaste, a natural toothpaste or water and baking soda.

• Don't put your baby to bed with a bottle. Liquid tends to pool around the teeth and bacteria then has all night to do its damage.

• Don't put juice or sugary drinks in bottles.

• Don't allow her to have lots of sweets.

• Begin regular dental check-ups from the age of two and a half.

• Until your child is six, make sure you help with teeth cleaning.

has a sore bottom and loose stools. If she is in pain, she will be fretful and may constantly put things in her mouth to bite on for some relief from the discomfort. You can help with this by providing her with carrot or apple sticks, crackers or teethers – the cooler the better – but be vigilant because babies can easily choose at this age.

In the late 1990s, fears were raised about the safety of brightly coloured vinyl (soft PVC) toys/teethers, which can leach toxic chemicals (phthalates) into children's mouths. As a result, certain large toy stores, supermarkets and manufacturers pledged to stop making or selling PVC toys and, in July 2005, the European Parliament permanently banned the use of certain toxic phthalates in toys, but these are still legal in most US states. At the very least, it is worth taking the precaution of buying only toys and teethers that are labelled as 'PVC-free' or 'phthalate-free'.

relief from painful teething

- Gentle massage around the jaw can reduce inflammation.

- If your child is in obvious pain or not sleeping, use an infant suspension containing paracetamol to control the pain and the fever.

- Two drops of clove oil diluted in eight to ten drops of olive or vegetable oil rubbed on the ruptured gum is very soothing. Test it on your own tongue first – it should tingle slightly but not burn. Dilute more if necessary.

- Weak camomile tea in a bottle or cup throughout the day can be very soothing.

WARNING As teething affects children in so many different ways, teeth get blamed for all sorts of problems around this time. Be careful that you do not miss signs of illness by putting all problems down to 'teething troubles'. A teething fever is generally mild. A temperature over 38°C (100°F) is unlikely to be caused by teething.

Early Foods

The food fun starts once your baby moves from weaning to eating solids. You may well have heard horror stories ranging from faddy eaters to food-spattered walls and ceilings but, like most things, with a positive approach and a little insider know-how, feeding your toddler can be good fun and, most importantly, it can lay the foundations for a lifetime of healthy eating.

Research now shows that a good diet established in childhood can help to prevent the risk of serious diseases common in later life, such as cancer, cardiovascular disease, diabetes and osteoporosis. In the shorter term, a varied and nutritious diet can help to ensure your child's healthy growth and development. So, if you want to give your child the best start in life, feed her a good, balanced diet.

Developing Good Eating Habits

By this, I don't mean good table manners – quite the contrary, in fact. I actually mean finding ways to encourage a healthy attitude to food and eating from the earliest days.

Food should be fun and it should be sociable, just as it is for adults. If you can feed your baby and then toddler alongside other members of the family, it is of great benefit to her. When small children sit down to eat and drink with other children and adults, it develops good social skills and behaviours, and encourages a positive association with eating and drinking. In addition, your child is also more likely to experiment with new foods if she sees other children and/or adults eating them.

It can be hard, especially if you have older children, to get everyone together for meals but it's so worthwhile if you can do it. Also try to avoid distractions, such as a television or radio playing in the same room, when you are feeding your toddler – let the meal and the company be the entertainment.

Fortunately, your child will take her lead from you. If you provide a good role model by being up-beat and positive about what she's about to eat, it's infectious. Young children are unable to spot overacting so play it

up as much as you like – lots of 'hmmm, delicious' and smacking of lips before offering food can convince the most reluctant eater to try a new or healthy food. Sampling it yourself first and reacting enthusiastically is equally persuasive.

One of the biggest traps for unwary parents is not allowing enough time for meals. Babies and toddlers need more time than adults to finish eating and drinking comfortably. You should allow a good fifteen minutes for a snack and at least thirty minutes for a meal. Small children need to eat every three hours, so when you offer a healthy snack between meals, time it so that you don't spoil her appetite for the next meal.

Eat Your Greens

Eating a variety of fruit and vegetables – home-grown or organic for preference – will give your child plenty of vitamins and minerals. Many are high in folic acid, vitamin C and potassium. They're also a good source of fibre and antioxidants. These are all important for your child's health not only now, but for the future.

Fruit and veg are also generally low-fat, low-calorie foods (provided you don't fry or roast them in lots of oil). So by choosing to eat them rather than less healthy

foods that are high in fat and added sugars, you can help your child to develop a taste for nutritious foods that will help her to maintain a healthier lifestyle and weight as she grows up.

Most babies and small children are happy to eat fruit and the sweeter vegetables, such as peas and carrots, but some baulk at stronger-flavoured green vegetables, such as broccoli and cabbage. To make sure your child has a wide variety of vegetables, you can disguise the less popular ones by hiding them in meals – chopped small in pasta sauces works a treat, for example.

It's a good idea to try to discourage your child from developing a taste for sugar. The natural sugar found in fruit and vegetables is absolutely fine but you should avoid adding sugar to the food or drinks you give your baby, not only from a health point of view but also because sugar can cause tooth decay. As with all things, moderation and common sense is the key. Provided the overall diet is well balanced – with adequate intakes of vitamins, minerals and fibre, and a suitable proportion of fat, protein and carbohydrate – moderate amounts of sugar are nutritionally acceptable.

One theory links a diet high in refined sugar with hyperactivity. Chromium, which is needed for the metabolism of sugar, is removed from sugar during the refining process. Without it, insulin is less effective in controlling blood sugar levels, and it has been suggested that this may lead to or exacerbate hyperactivity and behavioural problems, such as aggression and delinquency. However, despite a mountain of anecdotal material from parents, there is insufficient scientific evidence for this theory to be accepted by the medical establishment.

By comparison, the official advice regarding salt is unequivocal – we need to cut down on our salt intake – but that can be harder to achieve than you might think, since at least 60 per cent of the sodium in our diet comes from manufactured foods, such as bread, breakfast cereals and biscuits. Babies and children are less efficient than adults at excreting sodium, so they are much more vulnerable to excessive sodium intake, which can cause severe dehydration. This is why in the

UK the Food Standards Agency (FSA) recommends that parents cut down on the salt they use during cooking and at the table.

Regulating Salt Intake
When you start introducing solid foods, remember not to add salt to foods you give to your baby.

Avoid giving your baby any processed foods that aren't made specifically for babies, such as pasta sauces and breakfast cereals, because these can be high in salt.

If omitting salt from cooking and from the table, try using fresh or dried herbs and spices or garlic to

honey
It is a widely held view that honey is a preferential sweetening alternative to sugar because it is a natural product. Yet it is still a type of sugar and the amount you give to your child should be limited.

Honey should not be given to a baby until she is a year old because, very occasionally, it can contain a type of bacteria that can produce toxins in a baby's intestines. This can cause serious illness (infant botulism). After a baby is a year old, the intestine has matured and the bacteria cannot grow.

enhance or add extra flavour instead. If you find it impossible to omit salt from family cooking, choose a low-sodium salt alternative. These comprise half salt and half potassium. However, low-sodium salt should be avoided if you are diabetic or suffer from kidney disease.

Try to limit foods that are high in salt, such as cheese, bacon and sausages.

Check the nutritional information on food labels, bearing in mind that the figure may be given as sodium or sodium compounds, such as the preservative sodium nitrate, the flavour enhancer monosodium glutamate or sodium bicarbonate, which is a raising agent used in bakery products.

Try to choose foods that contain just a little sodium – 0.1g or less per 100g. A level teaspoon of salt weighs 5g. There are about 2.5g of sodium in 6g of salt, and it's the sodium that can lead to health problems. It might not sound a lot, but a food that contains 0.5g of sodium or more per 100g is considered to be high in sodium.

A Consumer Association investigation found that certain foods targeted at children, such as spaghetti hoops and baked beans, were less nutritionally sound than their adult counterparts. So check labelling carefully and do not be seduced by slogans such as 'ideal for lunch boxes'.

Try to cut down on the number of salty snacks your child has, such as crisps and biscuits. Provide low-salt snacks, such as dried fruit, raw vegetable sticks and fruit, as an alternative.

As with so much public-health advice, it is easy to overreact and to adopt stringent dietary measures for our children that are impossible to maintain. It is not possible or even desirable to cut sweets, biscuits, cakes and fast-foods from our children's diets entirely. It is more important to bear in mind that your overall aim is to give your child a varied and nutritious diet, to cut down on sugar and salt intake and to keep less healthy food 'treats' to a minimum.

food intolerance

As solids are introduced to an infant's diet, there can occasionally be an adverse reaction to certain foods, most commonly characterized by tummy upset. If your baby gets constipation, gas or diarrhoea after eating certain foods, it may be a sign of food intolerance. Unfortunately, the reaction can appear anywhere between an hour and two days after eating or drinking the offending food, which makes identification difficult. Food intolerances are rarely harmful and not as serious as a food allergy, where the reaction is instant and severe. Nonetheless, if you suspect a certain food is causing a problem, consult a doctor, midwife or nutritionist.

In the meantime, ease your baby's symptoms by infant tummy massage for gas (see page 144) and bicycling her legs for constipation. Remember to keep her hydrated if she has diarrhoea.

Babies are usually born with high levels of the enzyme lactase, so lactose intolerance (a reaction to cow's milk) usually begins only after the age of about two, as lactase production drops. If your toddler is identified as being lactose intolerant, give soya milk or hyperallergenic milk as a replacement for cow's milk.

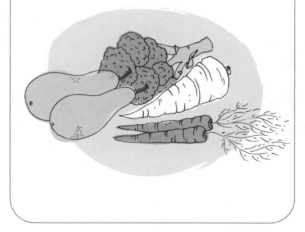

feeding at a glance

AGE	FOODS	FEEDING MILESTONES
Birth to 6 months	Breast milk and/or bottle formula	Rooting reflex (searches for food source) Sensitive gag reflex Tongue pushes out solid food
c. 6 months	Puréed fruit and vegetables, rice, cereal	Accepts solids from spoon or fingertip Sits in high chair
7–9 months	Greater variety of starter foods (see weaning, page 20)	Holds bottle Picks up finger foods and utensils Munches food
9–12 months	Lumpier consistency Poultry, yoghurt, cheese, pasta and breads	Holds trainer cup Getting messier as experiments Self-feeding improved
12–18 months	Most foods	Eats chopped/mashed family food Begins self-feeding with utensils Likes to do it herself
18–36 months	Toddler-sized portions of all foods	Molars appear so can chew Spoon-feeds herself quite successfully Needs creative feeding to hold attention

WARNING Babies and toddlers are prone to choking while they are getting accustomed to eating non-mashed foods, so stay vigilant. Be careful of large gobbets/chunks of food. Grapes and similarly sized items should be cut in half because these are particular choking hazards. Always make sure your toddler sits down to eat finger foods, rather than allowing her to run around or lie down while eating them.

Sleep

You will find that your newborn baby will take as much sleep as he needs, the only problem being that this may not coincide with when you'd like him to sleep. Newborn babies can sleep as much as 23 hours out of every 24, but it's also true to say that they may sleep as little as eight. On average, by their second week, a baby is sleeping between 16 and 18 hours per day, but plenty of babies are very wide of this average mark.

All that I can say with any certainty is that you will be experiencing broken nights and lack of sleep for many weeks to come, at least until your baby has established something of a routine that more closely coincides with your own. Initially, you may find that your baby sleeps a lot during the day and is awake more at night. Your baby has no control over his waking and sleeping at this early stage and that frustrating pattern may not reverse itself until he's about six weeks old.

It is something of a myth that most babies sleep through the night by eight weeks. Statistics show that by ten months, one in four babies are still not sleeping through the night. If another less-than-generous mother claims that her eight-week-old baby is sleeping through the night (the implication being why isn't yours?), your first reaction should be to try to ignore her ungracious behaviour and secondly, to question how she defines 'through the night'. If she considers a full-night's sleep to be from midnight until 6 a.m., she's doing well but that is not 'sleeping through' in many parents' eyes. Whatever you do, don't let it get you down, and remember you are not alone.

Most young babies are unable to sleep for long stretches because their brain is not sufficiently matured to regulate their sleep and because they need regular nourishment. It's optimistic to expect regular stretches of sleep of more than four hours before your baby is three months at the earliest.

Once you've got through the early days and have established something resembling a sleep routine, many parents continue to report concern over various aspects of their children's sleeping habits. A few of the more common complaints are discussed below.

Night-time Feeds

Many babies cannot make it through the night without a feed until they are in the latter part of their first year. Although no one likes a disturbed night, many mothers, especially those with older children, report that the night-time feed is the only occasion they have for a quiet, uninterrupted cuddle with the baby. Naturally, the baby enjoys the attention and, as a

During sleep, growth hormone is released
in humans and the growth of new cells
is faster.

result, stays awake long after his need for physical nourishment is satisfied.

Most mothers recognize that the trade-off for this intimate time with the baby is feeling tired in the morning. When you want to call a halt to this night-time indulgence, it is important that you complete the feed quietly, in the least time possible and with the minimum of attention. Then put the baby straight back to bed. This sounds a little callous but if you give your baby plenty of cuddles during the day, he will not miss out and it's the only way that he'll get the message that night-time feeding is for nourishment, not for fun.

Bedtime Rituals

Establishing a calming bedtime ritual will help your baby to recognize when play is over and it's time for sleep. Whatever the procedure you choose – a bath, a drink, a story, cuddles – it is important that you follow it routinely and that, once completed, you leave.

In this way, your baby will be reassured and, in theory, will then drop off to sleep on his own. If, on the contrary, you rough and tumble just before bedtime, it is unreasonable to expect your excited baby to lie down and go to sleep straightaway.

If the routine that evolves necessitates stroking, cuddling, singing, holding or comforting your baby until he's asleep, it is not surprising that the baby then expects the same treatment in order to fall back to sleep if he wakes in the night. Although this bedtime ritual might be acceptable at 7 p.m., it's rarely welcome in the middle of the night. Therefore, wherever possible, after completing a bedtime ritual, put your baby into his cot while he's still awake or drowsy. If he falls asleep by himself in the early

evening, he should have no problems doing the same when he awakes in the night.

Nonetheless, many parents fall into the trap of getting their babies to sleep by rocking or caressing them, and once this pattern has been established, it takes time and firmness of purpose to break the cycle. Diminish the routine gradually and in stages. If you normally nurse him to sleep, lay him in his cot while still holding his hand or stroking him. Then just sit next to the cot, moving the chair farther away each day until, eventually, you're sitting outside the room but on hand, in case he gets anxious. Once he is comfortable with each progression, move to the next stage until you are able to leave him without any fuss.

Leaving a Baby to Cry?

Opinion is divided on this emotive subject but, for many parents, letting your baby cry himself to sleep is usually too upsetting for all concerned.

The best method I have found is the gradual approach. This involves letting your baby cry for say

five minutes the first night before going to him, calming him and then leaving. After that, return every five minutes until your baby falls asleep. The next night, when he starts to cry, increase the time before going to him to six minutes, and subsequently return every six minutes. Each night the intervals increase up to a maximum of twenty minutes (if you can stand it) but most babies get the message long before they get anywhere near this length of time.

Sleeping in His Own Bed

In the western world, we do tend to expect our children to sleep in separate beds. However, in many cultures, babies and toddlers usually sleep with their parents while older siblings, of the same sex, sleep together. It is recognized that babies and young children sleep better when they share the parents' bed, but whether the same can be said of the parents is a moot point. Certainly, as long as you have not taken medication, drugs or alcohol, and if you are a non-smoker, it is safe to have the baby in bed with you. Nonetheless, it's always wise to keep the baby in the middle of the bed in case you accidentally knock him out or squash him between you and the wall, and you must be careful not to roll over and smother him.

If this arrangement suits you and your baby, then let it continue. However, if it ceases to please any one of you, a staggered withdrawal is recommended, rather than suddenly banishing your child from your presence at night. Keep the cot, or, if he's old enough, perhaps make up a bed, in your room for a short while before making the transition – and make sure that putting him in his own room does not seem like a form of punishment.

Daytime Sleep

At a year old, most babies still need a nap in the morning and the afternoon. The morning nap usually disappears next but the afternoon nap can continue until a child is four or even five, although for most, it disappears between the ages of two and three, when they drop it naturally.

Most parents face a dilemma at around this time. Should they get rid of the afternoon nap and put up with a cranky child who goes to sleep at night or should they allow a daytime nap and then, at bedtime, be faced with a lively child who has no intention of sleeping? Unfortunately, there is no right or wrong answer. It's called a 'no-win situation' and you just have to make a decision and try to be consistent.

Early Waking

If your child is waking and coming into your bedroom at an uncivilized hour of the morning, it may be because he has had sufficient rest and is no longer tired. In this

case, readjust his bedtime. As babies grow, so they need less sleep. Some toddlers and pre-school children need just eight to ten hours sleep to be rested and recharged.

If you change his bedtime and he still gets up too early, return him firmly to his room and allow him to play or read until it's time for the rest of the family to wake up. Placing an unfamiliar toy, something to drink or even a healthy snack by the bedside for him to find in the morning can be a good delaying tactic – and help you get some much-needed sleep.

sudden infant death syndrome

Although most of us know that it's irrational, as new parents we still harbour fears about Sudden Infant Death Syndrome (SIDS), more commonly known as cot death.

It is the fact that, in many cases, there are no known causes for the death of these babies that is so alarming to the new parent. However, the incidence of SIDS is low. In 2006, there were 321 deaths in babies under one in the UK and, in 2005, 0.51 cot deaths per 1,000 live births were recorded in the USA. The figures are falling year on year, so the chances of it happening to your baby must be kept in proportion.

Although it is important that you don't let worry about the possibility of a cot death ruin your enjoyment of your baby's first year, there are a few sensible precautions that every parent should take to reduce the risk:

• Place your baby on his back to sleep.

• Give up smoking during pregnancy – fathers too!

• Do not let anyone smoke in the same room as your baby.

• Do not let your baby get too hot (or too cold).

• Keep the baby's head uncovered – place your baby with his feet down at the foot of the cot.

• The safest place for your baby to sleep is in a cot in a room with you for the first six months.

• Do not share a bed with your baby if you have been drinking alcohol, take drugs or if you are a smoker.

• If your baby is unwell, seek medical advice promptly.

• Settling your baby to sleep (day and night) with a dummy can reduce the risk of cot death, even if the dummy falls out while your baby is asleep.

• For fuller details, get free leaflets from the Foundation for the Study of Infant Deaths (FSID) or the American SIDS Institute (see Useful Contacts, page 156).

Healthy Home Environment

Our natural instinct is to protect our children and to keep them safe from harm. However, environmental perils can be insidious, partly because the dangers are unseen and so easier to overlook, and partly because we may not even be aware of them. Then avoiding them can cause something of a dilemma. On the one hand, starting a family is the very time when you want hygiene to be at its optimum in your home, and yet you also want to protect your baby, and safeguard the environment, from the dangers of chemical pollution.

In this chapter, we look at some of the health and environmental precautions to think about when planning a nursery, which is, after all, the room in which your baby will spend so much of his early life (see page 42), and also focus on the number of cleaning products you use in your home and garden, and how they might affect your baby (see Pollutants, page 57, and Keeping House, page 52).

Some issues to be borne in mind when buying children's clothes, toiletries, nursery furnishings and baby-care equipment (see pages 63 and 49), are also considered.

Nursery Ecology

Babies sleep for a large proportion of the day, so it is fair to assume that they will spend a lot of time in their nursery, and since the young are especially vulnerable to environmental irritants, allergens and toxins, a great deal of care and attention should go into planning how best to make the room as safe for your baby as possible. You will want to take every precaution to guard against the possibility of your child developing asthma, for example, or any other disorder. The good news is that a plethora of environmentally sound products are available with which to decorate and furnish the nursery. They are just as attractive as synthetic products but pose much less, if any, health risks.

Do bear in mind, though, that important as these environmental considerations are, you should not worry about them to such an extent that it detracts from the pleasure of preparing the room for your new baby. Planning and shaping the nursery should be a delight for expectant or new parents, not a concern.

Buying healthy and environmentally friendly decorating and furnishing options is obviously the best choice for optimum health but even if you can implement just some of these recommendations, at least it's a step in the right direction.

Paints and Wallpaper

No matter how strong the urge to sand and repaint the baby's room, you should never do this yourself when pregnant. In old houses, sanding can disturb old lead paint, raising a toxic dust that you are likely to breathe in. It is widely known that lead can cross the barrier of the placenta, so not only could this dust give you lead poisoning, but it could potentially harm your unborn child as well.

In fact, lead-based paint has been banned in most western countries for many years but the danger from old and chipped lead paintwork in the home should not be underestimated.

In the UK and the United States, there are commercial companies who will come into your home and test walls, windowsills, doorjambs and house dust for the presence of lead. If unacceptable levels are found, or even traces for that matter, the company are equipped and qualified to remove the paint safely. Alternatively, you can get self-test kits from certain DIY stores to check whether your paintwork contains lead, but it will not tell you in what quantity.

> Infants have a respirational volume twice as large as an adult if compared weight by weight. So it's important that your child breathes the purest air possible.

If professional removal is not available to you, you can cover old paint with fresh non-toxic paint but be careful that it does not start to chip or flake, and is not repeatedly rubbed, because this could still release lead from the old paint layers underneath into the atmosphere. Never dry- or power-sand old paint. Lead poisoning is less likely if old paint is treated with a damp water-proof abrasive paper or with chemical stripper.

Most conventional, lead-free new paints and wood finishes still contain volatile organic compounds (VOCs), which readily vaporize into the air that we breathe. Their effects have been linked to complaints such as headaches, nausea, dizziness, nerve damage and, in extreme cases, liver and kidney disease. They are also suspected carcinogens. Low-VOC or VOC-free paints are readily available from DIY stores and other commercial outlets, so check labels.

If you are ardent about green issues, you can now find a wide range of eco-paints and natural varnishes available from specialist outlets and online distributors. These are designed as a healthier and environmentally friendlier alternative to using conventional paints and varnishes, and they include organic, milk (casein), water-based and natural types. They use primarily natural solvents, such as citrus and other plant oils, and are free of preservatives and biocides. These products tend to be more expensive than synthetic paints and often require more care and effort to mix and apply but, for those who want the best environmental option, these natural milk or organic paints are top of the list.

Unfortunately, if you are smugly thinking of avoiding paint altogether in preference for wallpaper and a border, this is actually not the sound environmental alternative you might imagine. Most wallpaper is not in fact made of paper but of vinyl, which can give off harmful chemical gases. And the adhesives for wall coverings are, unfortunately, worse still.

Nonetheless, as you've probably already guessed, there are environmentally friendly wallpapers and glues out there from which to choose. If these cannot be readily tracked down, another option may be to paint murals and stencils on to your baby's nursery walls using non-toxic paints, or alternatively, hang a natural cotton quilt or throw on the wall so that the painted or papered surface within the baby's reach is covered.

Carpets and Floor Coverings

If there is a history of allergies or asthma in the family, you may be best advised to avoid wall-to-wall carpets in the baby's room, since the dust mites that live in carpet pile are thought to worsen allergic conditions.

If the room is already carpeted and you prefer not to remove it, use topical treatments, such as anti-dust-mite sprays and a vacuum cleaner with a fine particle-trapping filter, to control allergens. To deodorize carpets naturally, sprinkle with baking soda,

leave for an hour, then vacuum. Should you decide to lay a new synthetic carpet, this should be done at least a couple of months before the baby is going to use the room because these give off toxic fumes for quite some time after installation. A better option is to stick with natural fibres, such as wool, but these carpets can cost up to twice as much as their synthetic counterparts, and some may still have synthetic backings. Tack down the carpet rather than gluing because the adhesives used for carpet laying are high in VOCs and give off toxic fumes.

Environmentally preferable alternatives to carpeting include untreated hardwood, cork tiling with natural sealant and true linoleum. It may also be worth looking for 'reclaimed' or 'recycled' timber that can be used for nursery flooring.

Soft Furnishings and Bedding

It makes good sense to choose natural and untreated fabrics, such as cotton and wool, for the sheets, blankets and cot bumpers with which your baby will come into direct contact.

Since a young baby sleeps in the region of sixteen to seventeen hours every day and a toddler sleeps around twelve, it stands to reason that your baby's regular sleeping place should be as comfortable and healthy as possible.

Biological contaminants, such as dust, dander, pollen, mould and mildew, cling to the fibres in

Organically grown cotton is now becoming more widely available and baby bedding and clothes made from this cotton will be appropriately labelled (see page 63).

Wool is warm, breathable and naturally water-resistant and flame-retardant, so it is an excellent choice for blankets or throws and mattress padding.

Natural fabrics, such as cotton, linen and hemp, are the best choices for your child's nursery curtains. If you choose synthetic fabrics, the heat and light coming through the window will cause them to break down and give off gases into the room.

Blinds made of aluminium, steel, wood and bamboo can be attractive in a baby's room, and as long as they have not been chemically finished (in which case allow them to aerate for a few days before installing), they are a healthy, non-allergenic option.

Although we are speaking here of decorating a new nursery, all these principles hold true, of course, for decorating the bedroom of a child of any age.

bedding materials. Asthma-inducing dust mites thrive on skin cells, dander and moisture in mattresses, sheets, pillows, cuddly toys, curtains and carpets. To minimize the risk of dust mites multiplying, you need to wash and dry all bedding at least every two weeks in very hot water (mites can survive in warm water) and regularly launder curtains and rugs. If this laundry regime pricks your environmental conscience, you could reduce the amount of detergent powder that you use for each load and substitute baking soda for half the normal dose.

When choosing natural fabrics, look for labels that say 'natural' or 'vegetable' dye rather than fabrics that have full chemical dyes. You should also be aware that, although we all think of cotton as a natural, breathable fabric, many cotton products we buy in the shops come from cotton that has been grown as a pesticide-intensive crop and is then bleached with chlorine-based chemicals before it is dyed.

Since the end of the Second World War, at least 75,000 new synthetic chemical compounds have been developed and released into the environment, the adverse effects of which are still largely unknown.

Natural Baby Equipment

There seems to be an inordinate amount of equipment to buy when your first baby comes along, some of which is essential, the rest less so. It's actually well worth speaking to other parents to find out which items they have used exhaustively and what has remained virtually untouched.

Certainly, for the nursery, you will want to buy a cot (crib) and probably a changing table (some parents swear by changing baby on the floor but it can become back-breaking after a while). You will also need to think about storage – a chest of drawers for clothes, possibly some wicker baskets, and shelves for toiletries and other essentials.

Nursery Furniture

It is such a charming idea to furnish the room with heirlooms that have been in the family for generations, but a word of caution is needed if you intend to use a hand-me-down cot.

Old cots do not always meet recent safety standards and may have structural weaknesses or design faults. Check for sturdy construction and avoid exposed fastenings with sharp edges. Avoid old mechanisms that can crush fingers, and cut-out designs that can entrap a child's head. Also satisfy yourself that it has not been painted with lead paint.

If you are buying new furniture for the nursery, whether it is a cot, changing table or chest of drawers, your best option environmentally is to choose solid hardwood with a non-toxic finish.

In the United States and the UK, look out for wooden products that have been certified by the Forest Stewardship Council (FSC). This means the manufacturers use approved management practices for maintaining ecological balance, such as selective logging that allows the forest to grow back and preserves biodiversity and wildlife habitat.

In general, timber described as rediscovered, reclaimed or recycled is a sound environmental option for nursery furniture.

Storage

Wicker stacking baskets for socks, vests and nappies are a good green alternative to plastic boxes. Similarly, wicker laundry baskets can replace plastic crates for storing toys.

Make sure, if you buy a toy or clothing chest, that it has a slow-closing, spring-loaded lid support. Avoid chests with latches that can trap an inquisitive toddler who climbs inside. Most new boxes are sold with ventilation holes or spaces for that very reason. So beware of antique or hand-me-down toy boxes and bedding chests that don't comply with these sensible safety precautions. If you want to use an old and treasured chest, fit a spring-loaded hinge or take the lid off altogether.

Baby Carriers and Backpacks

A wide variety of soft and hard carriers are available, designed for a spread of ages. Babies who cannot sit up on their own are best suited to soft slings that support their head and keep them close to your body (which babies find very comforting). You can carry older babies in slings that hang from the shoulder(s) and hold baby on your hip or front. Most soft carriers are available in 100 per cent natural cotton and a few come with a hood to protect your baby's head from sun or rain.

Babies of six months and older can sit in metal-framed backpacks that are great for hikes and walks – it's great to take your baby out in the fresh air and include him in family activities.

Prams and Strollers

From prams that double as car seats to the folding umbrella type of strollers – much favoured by parents of toddlers due to their manoeuvrability – the array of buggies from which to choose is almost baffling. Just one note of caution about clear PVC rain hoods – given the fears surrounding PVC, some parents prefer to use a material rain cape with an integral hood rather than allowing the baby to be cocooned in a plastic bubble.

greenfile

When buying a car seat, make sure it complies with the European or US safety standard.

Car Seats

Since 2006, it has been the driver's responsibility in Britain to ensure that children under fourteen years old are restrained correctly, in accordance with the law, on all car journeys. This applies to parents, grandparents, childminders and indeed anybody else driving a car with a child passenger.

Under UK law, children up to three years old must use a fitted car seat, booster seat or booster cushion that is appropriate for their age and weight in both the front and rear seats of all cars, vans and other goods vehicles at all times, or the driver risks prosecution.

Rear-facing seats are recommended for babies up to about nine months (c. 13kg or 29lb) and forward-facing child seats for infants weighing 9–18kg (20–40lb), roughly nine months to four and a half years old.

In the USA, the National Highways Traffic Safety Administration (NHTSA) recommends that children travel in appropriate car seats right up until they are eight years old, weigh 80lb or have grown to 4ft 9in. in height. When travelling through the US, you should adhere to the regulations of the state in which you are driving. If in doubt, follow the regulations of the most stringent state.

For all countries, don't forget to turn off airbags if you are putting your child in the front seat of the car, and bear in mind that once your child is in a forward-facing car seat, it is safest for her to travel in the rear seats of the car.

Of course, a child's car seat works effectively to protect your child only if it is properly secured and installed. According to a Which? survey, as many as seven out of ten child car seats are fitted incorrectly, which means that many children who are using good seats would be in serious danger if they were involved in a crash. So always follow installation instructions carefully and replace your child car seat after any accident that results in any damage to your car, however slight.

WARNING With any piece of baby equipment that folds or adjusts, such as a stroller, playpen, backpack or portable cot, make sure that you keep your child's fingers away from pinching mechanisms.

WARNING Rear-facing baby seats must not be used in a seat protected by a frontal airbag, unless the airbag has been deactivated.

Keeping House

Creating a home in which your child can grow up happily and healthily is something all parents hope to achieve. We aim to make the atmosphere in the family home as convivial and comfortable as possible – a space in which every family member feels relaxed and safe.

Despite the glut of make-over shows and glossy magazines that would have us believe otherwise, no single, correct formula exists for creating this 'ideal' modern family home. Naturally, your home will reflect your individual style, but irrespective of whether your house is a messy, busy space or an immaculate, minimalist homage to modern living, it needs to be maintained and kept clean.

So let's look at some ways in which green parents can 'keep house' in the most natural way possible.

Cleaning

Since you are reading a book on green parenting, you probably already shy away from some of the more potent commercial cleaners on the market. Nonetheless, even run-of-the-mill, perfumed proprietary brands can cause headaches, sneezing, sore throats, and irritated eyes, nose and skin in

Liquid detergents contain more harmful chemicals than powder or tablet equivalents.

susceptible youngsters. As for the environment, huge quantities of cleaning products and their packaging continue to fill our rubbish bins and eventually our landfill sites, bringing the inherent dangers of contamination of waterways, air and soil.

So it is worth reviewing the number of cleaning products you use in your home, cutting down where possible and avoiding any cleaners that carry caution warnings or are corrosive or caustic.

A whole host of safer, milder, eco-friendly cleaners are readily available these days – and, contrary to

chopping boards

Research by American microbiologists shows that the natural antibacterial properties of wooden chopping boards make them a safer option than plastic boards. Nonetheless, you must still be fastidious in the cleaning of all chopping boards, so scrub clean with hot soapy water and disinfect by spraying first with white distilled vinegar, then hydrogen peroxide and rinse well. Always keep boards used for vegetables and bread separate from those used for raw meat.

popular myth, they work. Alternatively, why not use the proven ingredients that your grandmothers used to clean the home? These are cheap and effective and they pose no health-threat to your child. Here's a taste to whet your appetite for home-made, all-round cleaning products:

* Bicarbonate of soda mixed with water makes a natural cleaning cream that cuts through grease and dirt on most surfaces in the kitchen and bathroom.
* One tablespoon of borax dissolved in 4 cups (about a litre) of warm water deodorizes and cleans the fridge.

* Remove limescale from taps by wrapping in a cloth soaked in white distilled vinegar. Leave for half an hour, then rinse clean.
* To clean and deodorize drains, put two tablespoons of bicarbonate of soda down the sink followed by half a cup of vinegar, leave for 20 minutes, then flush with cold water.

Disinfectants

Commercially bought disinfectants are licensed pesticides that kill bacteria, but you don't have to resort to chemical warfare to maintain a clean and safe home. Instead, you might like to consider using certain herbal oils and extracts as natural disinfectants in your home. Australian tea tree oil, pine oil and citrus seed extract are all known to have anti-fungal and antibacterial properties and can be used to wipe down surfaces, including in the nursery. However, they are not effective against harmful food bacteria, so do not rely on these in the kitchen or dining room.

Mould and Mildew

When cleaning the bathroom or shower-room, you probably pay particular attention to the mould and mildew that thrive in this moisture-rich room. Of course, you are right to be cautious of these microbes, which can lead to unpleasant respiratory problems, especially in children. However, rather than using proprietary anti-mould and mildew cleaning agents, which are also health hazards, use borax, vinegar or hydrogen peroxide (full-strength) to clean mould-covered walls and hangings. To prevent continued mould growth, take precautionary measures to keep down moisture in the home:

* Run extractor/exhaust fans, or open windows, particularly in the bathroom and kitchen.
* Use air conditioners or dehumidifiers in hot, humid climates – remembering to change filters and empty water tanks often.
* Regularly inspect plumbing for leaks.
* Keep rooms well-ventilated.

Wash-day Blues

As a general rule of thumb, you should attempt to cut down on the amount of detergent your family uses in the form of washing liquids and powders, washing-up liquids and dishwasher products.

Wherever possible, choose milder alternatives that are kinder to both the environment and health. You should also go for unscented varieties, because these reduce the risks of allergic reactions.

A useful tip when washing nappies, undergarments or nightwear is to add one cup of white distilled vinegar to the detergent dispenser of the washing machine for the final rinse cycle. This breaks down uric acid and any soapy residue, leaving them soft, fresh and fluffy.

Green Economy

To cut down on the amount of detergent powder used for each wash load, substitute bicarbonate of soda for half the normal dose of commercial powder. For heavily soiled loads, add half a cup of borax to your usual detergent to boost its efficacy, rather than using stronger detergents.

In fact, you can stop using fabric softeners completely since their sole purpose is to temporarily coat clothing fibres to prevent static cling. If your clothes are made of natural fibres, such as cotton, wool, linen and hemp, fabric conditioners or softeners are not necessary.

Finally, when replacing a washing machine or dishwasher, check the eco-friendliness of your new appliance. Whenever possible, choose the greenest machine available at the right price.

greenfile

Natural sunlight is a very good natural bleaching agent that does not harm the environment. So dry white baby clothes and towels in the sun.

WARNING Whether you choose commercial brands, natural products or make your own using natural ingredients, all cleaning goods must be kept well out of the reach of inquisitive little fingers and mouths. Even natural or safer cleaners can pose a health risk when ingested.

Pollutants

We now live in a sanitized, deodorized world where we all expect and demand the highest standards of hygiene and comfort for our modern family. In pursuit of this goal, the western home is packed full of cleaning products ranging from stain removers to air fresheners. Rather than the handful of general cleaning agents our grandmothers used, each modern product has a very specific and narrow purpose. This means that the average house may contain as many as 150 different products in the kitchen and bathroom alone, not to mention what we keep in our garden sheds and garages.

Although our levels of sanitation and hygiene are at the highest they have ever been, this progress has been bought at a high price. All the bleaches and disinfectants, the fertilizers and pesticides that we use routinely in our homes and gardens have a detrimental effect on our environment. And if that concept is rather too nebulous or far-from-home to affect your thinking, perhaps you should consider that these pollutants are also having a detrimental effect on the nation's health, and particularly that of our children.

Unfortunately, this is where the dichotomy lies. Having a baby or a young family in the house is the very time that you want your home to be at its most hygienic. You are never more scrupulous at scrubbing floors and surfaces and vacuuming carpets than when you have a crawling baby. Yet, infants are particularly susceptible to the harmful effects of pollutants from cleaning agents.

No one would suggest that you should not be fastidious about hygiene in the home and, if it came down to it and you had to choose between a clean house or a clear conscience, the hygienic home would win every time for the majority of parents. However, life is never that straightforward, is it?

You can still have a safe, clean home and yet give thought and attention to what's best for your children's health and the environment. However, this conscientious approach does take some application in terms of the time and energy you devote to choosing the right products and to both home and garden management.

It would be irresponsible scaremongering to suggest that your children's lives are at risk from

greenfile

Never mix commercial cleaners. Some contain ammonia and others contain chlorine bleach. These two agents mixed together form a toxic chlorine gas that can damage your lungs (it's very similar to the gas used in the First World War as a chemical weapon). Opt instead for traditional products that your grandmother might have used – they're just as efficient and much better for your child and the environment. For tips on natural cleaning agents, see Keeping House, page 52.

pollutants in the home. It is up to you to provide your children with a clean, safe environment in which to play and grow and you must achieve this however you see fit. However, if each of us does as much as we practically can towards reducing the effects of environmental pollution, it will contribute greatly not only to this worthy global cause, but to the individual health of our children.

Combustion Pollutants

This is the collective name for gases and particles that may be released into the air by the burning of fuels, such as natural gas, oil and wood. One of the main ones is carbon monoxide (CO), which is produced when carbon-based fuels don't burn fully. Exposure to combustion pollutants can increase the risk of cancer, respiratory infections, heart disease and retarded foetal development. Every year, many people undergo emergency treatment for CO poisoning, caused by inhaling CO produced by fuel-burning appliances, and there are even fatalities.

Appliances without ventilation or an exhaust flue, such as those found on certain gas cookers and paraffin (kerosene) heaters, are one of the major causes of combustion pollutants. Even vented appliances can be a problem if they are not regularly maintained and checked for leaks or blockages.

Unfortunately, many of the harmful particles and gases found in smoke and fuel emissions are undetectable by us, and so it is worth taking special precautions to safeguard our families:

* Install carbon monoxide alarms in rooms with gas heaters and appliances (but not right next to them in case a sudden surge gives a false reading), and outside the nursery, playroom and/or bedroom.
* Make sure gas cookers have good ventilation. Use an extractor hood and open windows when you cook.
* Never use charcoal barbecues and grills indoors.

electromagnetic fields

There is some controversy over whether or not exposure to electromagnetic fields (EFDs) caused by electrical currents from household appliances, power lines and conversion units can cause childhood cancers, such as leukaemia and brain tumours. The medical profession is divided and research so far has been inconclusive. However, until a definitive answer is reached, it may be wise to take the following health precautions:

Limit the time your children spend in front of VDUs and televisions.

Keep your child a safe distance from appliances in use, especially microwave ovens.

Turn off electrical appliances when not in use.

Keep electrical appliances in nursery and children's bedrooms to a bare minimum.

Don't use an electric blanket on a child's bed.

* Use electric radiant space heaters rather than paraffin or gas heaters.
* Ensure your home is energy efficient to reduce use of combustion heating.
* Limit use of open fires and wood-burning stoves, and keep chimney and flues clean and well maintained.

WARNING Never allow children to play on areas that have recently been treated with weed-killer.
Did you know that you can check the local air quality before letting your child play outside? This can be found in the newspaper, and is usually broadcast on local television and radio stations.

Radon Poisoning

Radon is a naturally occurring gas that is radioactive. It is particularly dangerous because it is odourless and colourless and impossible to detect without aid. No acute symptoms result from initial exposure to the gas, but continued exposure is a major cause of lung cancer. Test your house for radon levels using DIY test kits (preferably the long-term variety) or use a professional service. If detected, measures can be taken to reduce levels.

In the UK, a list of validated laboratories is available from www.defra.gov.uk/environment/radioactivity/radon and in the US, go to www.epa.gov/radon/radontest.html for approved centres.

Passive Smoking

The effects of passive smoking have been recognized as a major concern to health for many years and, as a result, legislation has been passed to curb smoking in public and workplaces. However, measures to reduce exposure to environmental tobacco smoke (ETS) in the home are virtually non-existent, despite the fact that the most vulnerable group in society, namely infants and young children, are mostly exposed to tobacco smoke at home.

In 1998, around 42 per cent of British children lived in a home where at least one person smoked. Although this number is falling, because adults are becoming more aware of the health risks to children posed by inhaling second-hand smoke, it remains relatively high for two reasons. Smoking is most common in the age groups that are most likely to have young children, i.e. 20–35 year olds, and young children spend most of their time at home and indoors.

While there is less scientific evidence about the detrimental effects of passive smoking than there is for active smoking, passive smoking has been linked to cot death, asthma, respiratory infections and ear disease in children. Quite apart from the health risks, a 2002 US report shows that children's mental development – reading and reasoning skills – is affected even at low levels of smoke exposure.

how environmental tobacco smoke affects the health of infants and children

In 2003, a survey found that 68 per cent of smokers said they do not smoke when children are in the room but most were unaware of the various ways in which passive smoking can affect children's health:

Asthma: Studies consistently show that asthma and wheezing in infancy and among schoolchildren is increased when at least one parent smokes. A review of 16 asthmatic patients also suggested that the severity of the disease is much greater in children exposed to smoking in the household.

Sudden infant death syndrome (SIDS): SIDS, commonly known as cot death, occurs more often in babies whose parents smoke. In fact, the risk of cot death approximately doubles if the mother smokes, independent of other factors.

Acute respiratory disease: The risk of bronchitis and pneumonia in infants up to the age of three is 57 per cent greater if parents smoke compared with non-smoking parents. Since respiratory disease in infancy is associated with chest disease in adulthood, the effect of early ETS exposure could have lifelong implications.

Ear disease: The risk of glue ear, a chronic middle-ear disease that commonly causes deafness in children, is increased by about one-third in children whose parents smoke.

Parents need to take action and responsibility, and evidence shows that the most reliable means of reducing your child's exposure to ETS is to stop smoking indoors, although I know this can be a hard habit to break. If you want to protect your child and you can't give up completely, the only thing you can do is smoke outside the house. Also, avoid smoking while driving with your child in the car.

In the Garden

The pesticides, fertilizers and herbicides that we use to keep our lawns looking lush and our gardens in tip-top condition have an extremely damaging effect on wildlife and the environment. Moreover, they pose a health risk to young children who crawl and roll on the ground that we've previously treated with these potent chemicals.

As parents, it's well worth looking into the possibility of using organic and traditional gardening methods and integrated pest management. Both options are kinder to our environment and to our children than going down the chemical path.

For example, rather than leaving harmful slug pellets (usually brightly coloured and highly attractive to toddlers) strewn around the flower beds, why not make a humane snail or slug trap to prevent damage to your plants (see right)? Other suggestions for a natural alternative to gardening pollutants include companion planting (plant three basil plants near a tomato plant to deter white fly and mosquitoes), introducing pest-eating wildlife (a ladybird can eat more than 5,000 aphids per year) and using natural barriers (slugs and snails dislike slithering over gritty surfaces so surround precious plants with a thick sprinkling of crushed egg shells, pine needles, coffee grounds or wood ash). In addition, you could try the commercial option of buying organic or chemical-free gardening products.

Making a natural slug trap

YOU WILL NEED
Large plastic drinks bottle
Knife or scissors
Trowel
Beer

METHOD
1 Cut off the bottom of the bottle.

2 Using the trowel to dig a hole, sink the base of the bottle into the soil.

3 Fill it with beer up to several centimetres deep.

4 Slugs and snails are attracted to the smell of the beer so they slither in and then get quietly squiffy before they drown.

5 Remember to empty (not pleasant but necessary) and replenish regularly.

Clothing and Baby Toiletries

Take a look at any catalogue for babywear and you can't help but be drawn to clothes that make your baby look cute and adorable. But at the back of your mind, you must also be conscious that your baby needs to be comfortable and protected.

The good news is that there are plenty of cute, fashionable clothes available for the green baby. Look for clothes made of natural fibres, preferably organic or undyed, untreated cotton or wool, silk and cashmere. Unlike synthetics, natural fibres breathe and are less chafing and irritating to a baby's sensitive skin.

Take care not to overdress your baby, because it's easy for them to overheat – better to use layers so you can adjust your baby's clothing according to the temperature. Physical signs of overheating include sweaty palms, underarms and necks, flushed faces and warm, red fingers and toes. Conversely, when your baby has become chilled, telltale signs include a bluish tinge to fingernails and no colour in the cheeks, but don't be misled – cool hands are normal in a comfortably dressed baby.

When it comes to infants' and children's sleepwear, it's sensible to choose fire-resistant and flame-retardant options. In the US, you must do so by law. Before these standards were adopted, a high number of infant fatalities were caused by pyjamas, nightdresses and dressing gowns going up in flames. In 1972 in the US, for example, up to sixty children a year died because their garments caught fire. By the 1990s, this figure had dropped to six per year, so it is an effective piece of legislation.

If you would prefer your baby to sleep in untreated cotton clothing, compromise by putting him in all-cotton underwear first and using standard treated nightwear on top.

Hand-knits

Babies and toddlers look fabulous in hand-knits. If you have relatives or friends who would like to knit for your child, encourage them to use untreated wools. If you want to go the whole hog, go for untreated and undyed wools, which are usually available in off-white, grey and brown. You can find wools that have been coloured using vegetable dyes if you want a wider range of colours.

If your child's skin is sensitive to wool, suggest your knitter uses merino, silk and cashmere yarns, which are less coarse than wool, and find patterns incorporating pointelle or stockinette stitches, which give a finer feel.

Baby Toiletries

There's nothing quite as wonderful as a baby's skin, which is why some experts recommend using nothing stronger than warm water and a cloth on it. For those who prefer to use babycare products, the rule of thumb is always go for the mildest and purest option.

Choose a baby soap that uses natural ingredients, such as an olive-oil based soap. Avoid antibacterial and highly-scented soaps, which are too harsh for babies. Baby shampoo and bubble baths are generally milder than those for adults, so don't be tempted to let her splash in some of your own bath products.

If your baby has an adverse skin reaction to any toiletries, rinse off well using clean, warm water and, obviously, don't use that product near your child again. In the rare event of a more serious reaction, such as watering eyes, reddened skin and breathing difficulties, remove your infant from the bath and call a doctor immediately.

How to bath your newborn baby

1 Before you start, make sure the room is warm, and gather together all the items you will need, namely a baby bath, a thick towel to place under your baby and pad against the bath's hard surface, cotton flannels, a warm hooded towel and a bath thermometer (optional).

2 Place the baby bath on a steady tabletop, on the floor or even inside the big bath.

3 Test the bath water on your wrist to make certain that it's comfortably warm but not hot.

4 Undress your baby and wrap her in a towel. Supporting her body along one forearm, with the back of her head resting in your hand and her bottom securely tucked between your elbow and ribs, gently rinse her face and hair, holding her head over the bath.

5 Now, take off the towel and gradually lower her into the water, keeping one forearm behind her shoulders so that her head rests on your wrist while that hand holds her around the shoulder and armpit.

6 Gently clean from neck to bottom, being especially careful around the stump of the umbilical cord, and gently splash warm water over her chest, tummy and legs. Make sure you have a secure grip – one hand around her shoulders and the other under her bottom, holding her thigh – before lifting her out.

WARNING Never let go of a baby in the bath, and never leave a young child unattended since drowning can occur in less than 25mm of water.

Natural Learning

3

Naturally, every parent wants to give their child the very best education possible to prepare him for life as an adult in the wider world, but it should not be assumed that good exam results are the best yardstick of a child's learning.

To the uninitiated, young children at play appear carefree and haphazard in what they're doing, but in fact, they're learning through their games and through imitation. That does not mean that if you toss a Rubik's cube into your child's cot from his earliest days, you'll be guaranteed the next Einstein. Natural learning just means that children develop and progress through recognized stages at the pace that suits them. A child can, through play, learn without conscious effort.

This learning takes place without your intervention but it does require your understanding and support, and being able to communicate before your child is fully articulate is a huge advantage in this regard. Interpreting body language (see page 87) is a useful skill for both parent and child.

As long as you offer your child plenty of opportunities, resources and an environment that's conducive to creative play (see Creating a Positive Learning Environment, page 68 and Emotional Intelligence, page 81), learning becomes a natural part of his childhood.

When it comes to more formal pre-school care and education and finally to mainstream schooling, should you choose to go down that route, parents can quail at the enormity of the decisions they face. In reality, finances, geographical location and working hours influence the choices made but it's worth taking some other considerations into account (see Early Childcare Provisions, page 72, and Home Schooling, page 78).

Creating a Positive Learning Environment

If left to her own devices, a child's natural learning ability will enable her to master complicated skills, such as walking and talking, when she is ready. Her innate curiosity and desire to explore will inform her about her world and, as she busies herself with the serious business of play, you have only to marvel at this learning experience unfolding before your eyes.

Moreover, if you lend your encouragement and support to her endeavours, the spectrum of skills and learning she will acquire quite happily and without undue effort is inexhaustible.

Pressure to Conform

With the emphasis today on equipping our offspring for the challenges of the twenty-first century, many parents feel an immoderate pressure to hustle their young children towards gaining academic qualifications. We buy home computers for three-year-olds to give them a head-start. We pressurize pre-school kids to learn to read and write. Hot-housing infants to pass entrance exams for desirable schools is far from uncommon.

In the main, such endeavours are undertaken with the best of intentions. Most parents simply want to give their children an advantage in life, and feel that educating them from an early age will set them up for good prospects at school and in later life.

However, this pressure on our children to perform may draw a child too quickly into adult preoccupations and cut short the full experience of childhood. It puts all the emphasis on academic achievement and flies in the face of all we know about how children learn naturally.

Unlike adults, who are analytical and intellectual, a child's method of learning is through imitation and repetition. She acts and from that, reflection stirs. Her learning comes initially from movement and later becomes cognitive.

For a child to develop normally, she needs to be exposed to a rich tapestry of sensory experiences. Whether it is a parent or a teacher, an educator's task is to awaken and nourish a child's learning potential and not just to inform and instruct.

Setting the Scene

Parents create the culture in which a child grows and learns. Irrespective of your personal style, home should be a convivial place in which your child has plenty of opportunity and space for free-flowing play, for making things and for drawing. Naturally, you have to provide the resources for this play but they do not have to be expensive or sophisticated. Scrap paper is perfectly adequate, and if finances won't stretch to modelling materials like clay or modelling dough, make your own (see page 70). If weather permits, why not go outside?

---

greenfile

Objects and creatures your child sees in nature offer great scope for counting games as she becomes aware of numbers. So, ask your toddler, how many legs does a beetle have? How many legs does a cat have? How many wings does a bird have? How many petals does a tulip have?

Home-made modelling dough

YOU WILL NEED

Cream of tartar, 2 teaspoons
Plain flour, 1 cup
Salt, ½ cup
Oil, 1 tablespoon
Water, 1 cup
Food colouring (optional)

METHOD

1 In a saucepan over a low heat, mix all the ingredients except the food colouring, to form a smooth paste.

2 Keep stirring until the dough forms a ball.

3 Allow to cool down slightly, then knead by hand for a few minutes.

If you want the dough to be coloured, mix the food colouring with the water before adding it to the flour and salt. Alternatively, add the food colouring a few drops at a time at the kneading stage.

4 Store in an airtight container in the fridge.

Making mud pies in the garden can fulfil the same purpose as playing with expensive modelling clay. It's more a question of approach than anything else.

The point most parents miss is that a child is learning all the time. She makes no distinction between learning and playing. There is no need to set up special learning opportunities if you acknowledge that she is learning about life at every moment. By including her in your own activities, she will learn through imitation. For example, you cannot instil moral fortitude in your children by lecturing them. They will pick up rights and wrongs from your actions and reactions towards others and to certain events.

The best early learning environment you can provide for your child is one in which she can explore for herself. She wants and needs to manage her own learning but she requires your help for encouragement and confidence-building. Educationalists define this as a 'coaching' role for parents – you provide examples for your child to copy and allow her to learn without constant interruption. Through imitation, she will acquire the attitudes and skills necessary for successful learning throughout life.

'You are the bows from which your children as living arrows are sent forth.'
Kahlil Gibran

helping your child to learn

Give her love and a sense of self-esteem.

Encourage her and have confidence in her ability to succeed.

Encourage persistence not mastery.

Never threaten to withdraw love if she fails to achieve goals.

Listen to her ideas.

Recognize her right to her own feelings and give her a chance to express them.

Give her experiences from which to learn.

Know when not to interfere.

Encourage your child to finish what she starts.

Give her freedom to make her own mistakes and to learn from them.

Never punish mistakes.

Don't be too busy for her.

Stop telling her what she's doing wrong.

Share and show pride in her achievements.

You can stimulate your child's natural curiosity and desire to learn by being interested in whatever she shows you and talking about it with her. This reassurance allows your child to make sense of the world around her.

A child needs to have successes but she must also be allowed to make her own mistakes, although you should keep some perspective in this. Letting her do something dangerous or life-threatening so she 'learns a lesson' is missing the point and, more importantly, is downright irresponsible. What it means is that when she's ready to learn a new skill, you should resist doing it for her or interfering unasked. It may be difficult and time consuming, it may well be frustrating for her (and you), but once mastered, she'll gain enormous satisfaction from her achievement. She will also learn that perseverance pays off and this will affect her approach to all learning in later life.

Future Schooling

Looking ahead, once your child is part of the education system, you can continue to support her by showing an interest in everything that she does at nursery school and by getting involved as much as possible in organized activities and her work projects.

In addition, you can continue to provide learning opportunities at home. It doesn't have to be anything overtly educational, as we've already seen. Encouraging her to help you with general chores and activities in the home and garden provides an opportunity to learn through imitation.

Try to keep in mind that there is no race to acquire the early skills she will learn at school, such as reading and writing. It is more important that she comes to enjoy reading when she's ready. You can help by reading to her, sharing books with her and taking her to the library, for example.

Give her individual attention together with affection in abundance, and your child cannot fail to learn effectively.

Early Childcare Provisions

Entrusting your child to the care of others is always a fraught and worrying choice for parents. It is important that you choose the best option for your child's temperament from the wide range of childcare options available, and that you do so at the right stage in her development. A few children are not suited to pre-school provisions, but for the majority of young children, finding the right care giver can bring benefits in terms of social, emotional and educational development.

Of course, for many parents, the need to work means that pre-school childcare provisions are an essential requirement rather than an option. For others, the idea of extending their child's experience and socialization prompts them to look at early education services. For a diminishing number of parents, the family home is considered the only natural place for young children to learn and experience life until they are ready to start school.

In most developed countries, the options available to parents fall roughly into two categories: services where the primary concern is the care, safety and well-being of the child; and services that also provide some kind of educational experience for an older, pre-school child.

Caring Options

If you are a working parent looking for flexible care in a family setting, you will probably end up trying to choose between a childminder and a nanny.

Childminders are often young mums themselves who offer childcare for other children from a few months old to school age. A good childminder will offer your child a warm relationship in her own family setting. Often, a childminder will do all the things with your child that she would normally do with her own, and some children, especially a lone child, can benefit from mixing regularly with other youngsters of various ages.

Rather than disrupt a child by taking her from her own environment, some parents prefer the more costly option of having a nanny who comes into their home to look after their child. A nanny performs the same function as a childminder and often develops a loving bond with the child in her care.

Since your child could be spending quite a lot of time with your chosen care giver and a loving attachment often forms, it's important to try to maintain some continuity. If you keep changing the childminder or nanny, it can be very upsetting for your child and may cause her to become anxious, unhappy or insecure. So you must be very careful how you select your care giver in the first place (see overleaf).

Another option for early childcare is a day nursery. These are staffed by professionals who look after babies and young children during working hours. The main purpose of a nursery is the well-being and care of the child but some also offer activities that can promote language, reading and writing skills, particularly for the older children, and have other educational value.

Private individuals, local authorities, companies or voluntary groups can run day nurseries. You usually

Your child's attachment to you first and foremost is at its strongest between the ages of six months and a year. So try to introduce childcare before your baby is four or five months old or after the age of about fifteen months.

A child's fear of unfamiliar children peaks at around twenty months, so be aware of this if introducing her to a creche or nursery at this time.

choosing a care giver

The person chosen should have a style of caring that is broadly similar to your own.

Introduce a prospective care giver to your child to see how they interact.

Always check credentials and take up references.

You must feel comfortable with, and have confidence in, your child's care giver. Your child will pick up on any unease.

You must feel able to tell the care giver if anything concerns you.

Make sure the care giver knows all about your child's temperament, likes and dislikes and idiosyncrasies – and keep him/her updated, because these change regularly.

Always believe and follow up any complaints or misgivings expressed by your child about her care giver.

Remember to trust your instincts – your intuition is more reliable than paper qualifications – and be thorough. After all, you are entrusting the care of your beloved child to this individual or organization – you have a right to satisfy yourself completely before handing your child's temporary well-being to them.

have the option of sending your child part-time or every day of the week and this can be useful if you don't need childcare for enough hours to make it economically worthwhile for a childminder or nanny.

Playgroups and Toddler Groups

For a parent who does not work or who works part-time, playgroups or parent and toddler groups can be a good option. Playgroups are usually run by one or two paid staff with the help of some parent volunteers, and are equipped with modelling dough, crafts, puzzles and other toys, catering for children between two-and-a-half and five years old. Your child can attend one or more sessions a week, usually on her own (once she's settled in), but with you if you both prefer.

Mother and toddler groups are organized by parents and usually meet once a week. The children play together while the parents have a chance to chat and relax with others in a similar situation. These groups rarely offer organized activities and creative play. However, both options give babies and toddlers a chance for social interaction with other children.

Nursery and Kindergarten

These are staffed by qualified professionals who provide the children with developmentally and age-appropriate activities five mornings or five afternoons a week. The nursery school may be privately or state run or it may be attached to a primary school, but the ratio of adult to child is usually about half that of a school classroom.

A good nursery school should offer a child an opportunity:

* for hands-on involvement
* to do what interests her
* to discuss with an adult what she'd like to do, how to do it and what materials to use
* to learn by experiment
* to interact with other children and adults
* to be creative, inventive and imaginative
* to take the initiative and responsibility for tasks.

There is some evidence to suggest that a good nursery education can help a child in later life and that those who have had good experiences of a pre-school group tend to be more resilient, more confident and better able to deal with social situations. They are also better equipped to plan their work independently.

If the services offered have each child's best interests at heart, and are not solely motivated by financial gain, any of these options can bring great benefits to a child and to parents. However, it doesn't matter how good the pre-school provision may be, there will always be a few children who are simply not ready or suited to a busy group environment, or who are not ready to be separated from their parents. Tears on separation are natural for many children but if your child remains unhappy or anxious, you may have chosen the wrong option for her, or perhaps she is just not yet ready for this move.

greenfile

One of the most well-known styles of alternative nursery schooling is the Montessori system, which is based on the philosophy of Maria Montessori, who was born in 1870 in Italy. Her methods are founded on the idea that children learn from self-motivated activity within a highly structured environment. She believed that 'play is child's work' and that young children experience periods in their development when certain concepts or skills are more easily procured. Therefore, the Montessori approach offers prepared materials in a planned sequence so that children can work with a high level of independence to attain specific skills and concepts at the right time.

In Britain in 2005, both parents worked in 52 per cent of families with children. In the US, 78 per cent of children have at least one parent working full-time.

Home Schooling

When you look at your baby or toddler, starting school seems like an age away but you'd be surprised how quickly it comes around. Depending on where you live, there's every chance that you've already considered putting your child's name down at the best school in the area but, if there is no school that you're happy with or if you are dissatisfied with the education system in general, you could consider home schooling.

Many parents are surprised to learn that although education is compulsory from the age of five in the UK, schooling is not. The responsibility for a child's education falls to the parents and, although the vast majority choose to delegate this to schools, some opt to educate their children at home – and the number is growing. In the UK, official estimates say that up to 50,000 families are now home-schoolers, and in 2007, 80 per cent of education authorities reported a huge increase in the number of children they knew were being home educated. Over a million families in the USA educate their children at home – that's roughly 2.2 per cent of American students.

Some families resort to home-based schooling because their kids have had an unhappy or unsuccessful experience in a traditional school, although for most, they plan to educate their children at home from the outset.

Getting Started

Type 'home schooling' into any internet search engine and you will see numerous links ranging from those offering learning programmes to small individual sites or blogs that offer their own personal experiences of home education.

---

greenfile

One of the beauties of home schooling is that you can build in daily activities that get your child into the fresh air, such as gardening or going on nature trails. Similarly, regular excursions are popular, for example, visiting museums or places of interest. Some parents encourage their home-schooled children to join local community projects. Proponents of home schooling suggest that all of these activities help to give a child a more rounded, fuller education.

As well as online learning sites, a wealth of resource material is available, including CD-ROMs on most academic subjects, text books and general interest books. Initially, families often prefer the comfort of following a set package – some of these even include a personal tutor in a particular subject – but there is no legal requirement to do so.

Common Reservations

Some parents naturally have misgivings about whether home education will be good for their children, as well as their own ability to provide it. Here are some of the usual topics of concern.

Socialization: Supporters of home-based education maintain that learning activities in the community give children more social contacts with people of all ages and more variety. It encourages autonomy and the development of self-directed learning.

Taking exams: Formal testing is not required but children can still be entered for exams when the time comes, either as a private candidate, by following a correspondence course, or by enrolling part-time at a Further Education College.

'I'm not a teacher': Don't worry, the majority of home educators are not qualified teachers. You simply have to use your initiative and take advantage of the resources and support available – and there is plenty – to help you to work on just what you want, when you want, with your child.

Special needs: If your child has special needs, this is not an obstacle to home education. The process is exactly the same as for any other child, and the Local Authority or school, if you are withdrawing her, cannot legally refuse, although they may make further enquiries about your continuing educational provision for your child.

Einstein proposed that imagination was more important than knowledge in our changing world.

arguments for and against home schooling

FOR

You spend the majority of your time with your children and see them develop and grow.

Your child mixes with people of various ages which prepares her for the varied interactions of life.

There is much more flexibility in what your child learns and when.

The classroom is predominantly one-way communication whereas home-based education involves meaningful interchange.

You set the educational objectives, which can be different for each child if you are teaching more than one.

Home-educated children have fewer behavioural problems.

AGAINST

You have no opportunity to develop your own career if you're engaged in the full-time education of your children.

Your child may have less opportunity for interaction or social life with her peers.

It's difficult to organize team games and science experiments, or to provide the materials found in schools.

If your child does not take exams, there are no formal, recognizable qualifications to show future employers.

Emotional Intelligence

Every parent wants their child to do well and to prosper and, as a result, most of us place considerable importance on their education and learning. However, it should come as no surprise that mental capacity is not the only key to success. In fact, new findings show that your child's emotional intelligence may be more important than his IQ in determining how well he does in overcoming the challenges of life and in his relationships with others.

Most of us are familiar with the intelligence quotient (IQ) method of assessing a person's intellect and most of us are aware that if you have a high IQ, you are expected to achieve good academic results. With our modern preoccupation with mental ability, we assume a high IQ rating is equable with success but this is not necessarily the case. Plenty of youngsters who are considered cerebrally gifted fail to live up to their early promise.

One of the reasons for this is that IQ as a form of assessment takes into account certain aspects of your child's ability only. Success, whether you measure it in terms of qualifications, career attainment or personal fulfilment, is dependent on more than just brains. The limitations of IQ ratings are starting to be acknowledged and educators are now considering concepts such as 'multiple intelligence'. Nonetheless, it is still mental capacity and cognitive development that are given paramount importance in the education systems of the developed world at the moment.

A New Approach

Since the early 1990s, attempts have been made to change that attitude. In 1990, Americans Peter Salovey and John Mayer published an emotional intelligence (EI) ability test, having established that there are other factors that are much more likely to lead to success in life than IQ. Since then, Mayer and Salovey have led the scientific development of the theory behind emotional intelligence and its measurement.

In 1995, a fellow American, Daniel Goleman, published a book entitled *Emotional Intelligence,* that built on Salovey and Mayer's work, and in it he summed up the factors that contribute to EI, which are present to varying degrees in all our children. The qualities that he recognized as forming EI are:

* Self-awareness
* Empathy
* Impulse control
* Self-motivation
* Self-discipline
* Compassion
* Altruism

The good news for parents is that we can help to nurture and strengthen the characteristics of emotional intelligence from the earliest age.

If you consider that nearly all the characteristics that Goleman uses to measure emotional intelligence are essential to forming good relationships, it comes as no surprise to learn that a child's emotional development inevitably rests, in no small measure, on the emotional stability of the parent(s). Therefore, if you relate well to each other and share positive relationships with other people in your lives, there is every chance that your offspring will exhibit similar skills in their own relationships.

Attunement to the mother and/or father is the keystone to much of a child's early emotional development. This means that not only must you register what your child is experiencing but that you should also be able to let your child know that you have a sense of what he is going through.

impulse-control

An experiment was carried out with three- and four-year-olds whereby each was given a choice of having two marshmallows if they waited fifteen minutes before eating them, or one marshmallow if they ate it straightaway.

Ten years later, the group was revisited at high school. Those who had resisted temptation and waited for two marshmallows were found to be more self-confident and more socially competent whereas the children who had opted for the instantaneous pleasure of one marshmallow had considerably fewer desirable attributes, tended to overreact to irritations, and more often provoked arguments and fights.

Perhaps, as parents, the lesson to learn from this experiment is that we should reinforce in our children the advantages of having some control over our overwhelming desires.

Innate Empathy

For a child to develop positive, considerate behaviour, he has to recognize and appreciate the feelings of others. Incredibly, this capacity is now known to be present in newborn babies, who cry when they hear another baby in distress. Children appear to be born with an innate ability to understand others and this uniquely human faculty is a capacity on which parents can build. As your child grows, his understanding of others will gradually increase, based on observing other people's actions and responses.

If children are brought up in an atmosphere where they see that their parents and others are willing to be of help to someone in distress, they are more likely to be empathetic themselves as they grow up.

Following the principle of parents acting as models for their children's behaviour, if a child sees a parent habitually reacting with a violent response when angered, that child has an increased chance of using violence to achieve his own ends. Equally, if a child has been shown the value of pausing and considering the implications of an act and then negotiating a settlement, he is more likely to exhibit impulse-control and, as a result, to lead a more peaceable existence.

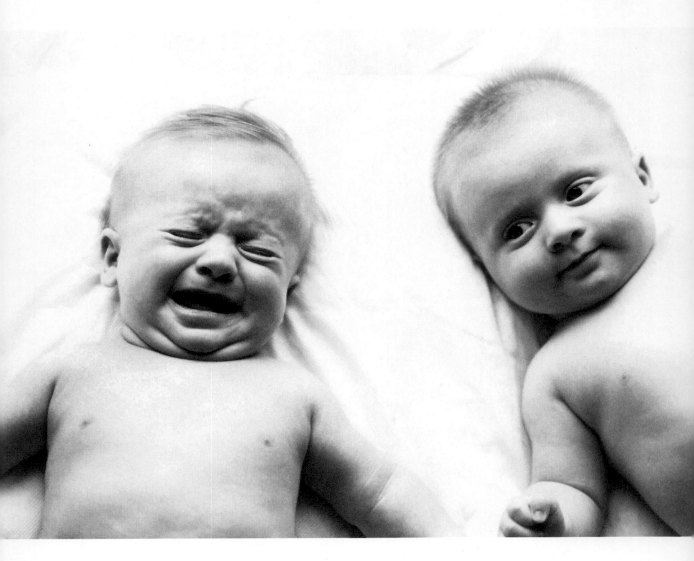

Body Language

The very first communications between a parent and a child rely not on words but on physical expressions of love and intimacy. A baby or small child does not understand your words but he is very well attuned to your expressions and gestures. He interprets your meaning and intent, your moods and your reactions from your physical responses, facial expressions and the tone of your voice. As a result, a child is generally much more conscious of, and better able to interpret, body language than an adult.

It was not until the twentieth century that scientists were able to measure what children seem to know intuitively, i.e. that body language plays a vital part in the way humans communicate. In fact, the American anthropologist, Dr Ray Birdwhistel, established that communication was made up of:

    7% words
    23% tone of voice
    35% facial expression
    35% gestures

Since children are so adept at reading our unspoken meaning, it is useful to think about how we communicate non-verbally if we are to create a better rapport with them. If you know that you can consciously use gestures and exaggerated expressions to get a message across to a small child, just think what you might be saying unconsciously.

Actions Speak Louder than Words

It is no good listlessly calling from the kitchen to your three-year-old in the sitting room that it's time to start tidying up and then being surprised when you go in a few minutes later and discover that nothing has been done. It is vital that you mean what you say when you speak to your child, if you want to get the right response (or any response at all for that matter). If your words are contradicted by your body language, you will give off a confused message and it will have a limited effect, if any.

In this case, what tends to happen is that your child fails to react to your mixed message and ignores you until you become so frustrated and annoyed that your message finally evolves into a form that is in keeping with your true feelings. At this point, the message becomes clear, or congruent in the technical vernacular, and so the child takes heed. So, when

next the vicar comes to tea, don't expect your grinning, butter-smeared darling to remove his hands from the vicar's vestments, if you are smiling sweetly when you gently tell him to do so. Until your face and tone reflect your steely resolve, there's little hope of him releasing the vicar from his greasy grip.

Your demeanour must give the message that you have no doubt that your child will do as you ask. In this way, you leave less chance for debate or negative reaction and you increase the probability of getting the result you want.

Of course, the reverse of this is equally true. If you are lavishly praising your child's latest work of art with barely a glance in the right direction and scarcely hidden disinterest, he will soon realize that your words are hollow and that you don't really care, and the implications of that are clear for us all to see.

Your body language is also essential if you are to be taken seriously. There is no point at all in taking a stand if you don't look like you mean it. Any sign of wavering and your child will exploit the weakness and badger you until you cave in. Say no with conviction.

Tuning in to Your Child

Without thinking about it, when adults are relaxed, they each mirror the other's behaviour to express empathy. So, when one friend sits down, the other does the same; if one speaks in a soft tone, the other speaks more quietly, too. This device can be used in certain circumstances with children to show empathy in a difficult situation.

If your child is upset and doesn't want to talk, sit near him in a similar pose, hunched or supine. If he hugs his knees, you hug yours. In this way, without invasion, you are showing that you understand and sympathize with what he is feeling. Once he is reassured that you are not going to interfere, either physically or emotionally, he will start to calm down and relax, and he may well want to talk again; or he may simply prefer some physical comfort.

Just as your child will pick up a mixed message if your body language belies what you say, you can sometimes read your child's actions better than his words. If he is starting to get worked up and angry, and his behaviour is becoming hostile, watch closely to see if his face is showing signs of being upset, hurt or misunderstood. If you suspect that he really wants you to comfort him although his actions suggest that he's trying to alienate you, utter a few words of understanding and comfort. You may well find that he is relieved to be understood and dissolves into floods of tears of relief and genuine upset. Sometimes children's behaviour is just posturing, and often their body language is the clue to when they are being frauds. Watch out for it, because it can save some unnecessary confrontations.

greenfile

Actions speak louder than words – so give your child a hug when you tell him that you love him.

using body language to best effect

When your child is talking to you, make sure you give him your full attention.

Put yourself on the same level as your child when you are speaking to each other, either by crouching down, lifting him up or sitting him on your knee.

Make sure you're in the same room, and preferably have eye contact, when you ask your child to do something.

Listen to what your child has to say but also be aware of his body language and make sure the two don't conflict.

Adjust your conversation to the speed and volume of your child.

Make sure your words reflect how you feel and that your message is clear.

Play and Creativity

Play and creativity are vitally important in your child's early years. Whether it is in fantasy play or with toys specifically designed to develop cognitive skills, it is through the medium of play that, in the first two years of his life, your child will unconsciously build up his intellectual powers. After the age of two, role play takes on a greater significance in your child's life, and from as early as twenty months, he might start to act out events from his daily life, or pretend a building block is a car.

In this chapter we will explore how creative play (see page 96) brings benefits, such as better concentration, improved language development and an enlightened approach to problem solving, and we celebrate the inestimable advantages of allowing your child to enjoy his gift of imagination (see Imaginary Play, page 100).

Whatever activity your child is engaged in, whether it's creative art (see page 108), music and movement (see page 92) or physical games (see page 110), he learns best and most easily when he is allowed to participate actively and fully. He must feel he is doing it himself.

Although it is tempting to try to hasten your child's progress, there is no need for him to learn quickly. Allowing him to inhabit his fantasy world as well as the real one will help him to enjoy a rich flow of imaginative ideas and spontaneous inspiration. You can play an active role in this, not only by providing the opportunities for your child to enjoy uninterrupted creative play, but also by telling him bedtime stories (see page 104).

Dance, Music and Movement

Musicality is not something that children do or do not possess. All children love to move in time to music and to bang a drum or shake a rattle. This is the foundation stone for creativity in music, dance and movement. Communication amounts to far more than just verbal dialogue, and children often find that the freedom to express themselves through dance, music and movement is a liberating and joyful experience.

Movement

Movement is a child's first language. It is through movement that a child explores the world, orientates herself and learns to coordinate eyes and body. She can also communicate through her body movements, her posture and gestures telling you much of what she is feeling long before she is able to tell you in words (see Body Language, page 87).

For a toddler, movement and communication are inextricably linked. If you ask a two-year-old to say 'hand', she will automatically wave it as she articulates the word. This is because children learn by doing. A pre-school child needs to have plenty of activity, such as running, hopping, rolling, skipping and jumping, to improve her gross motor skills and to prime the system for the fine muscle skills that will follow.

Not only is it true that movement helps to develop spatial awareness, a sense of direction and control of balance, but it is also believed that until a child starts to develop control of movement, she will not be able to master language as an independent skill.

Dance

It doesn't matter what type of music they hear, children always respond with the same uninhibited delight. They leap around and jig about, and whether or not they appear to be in time is immaterial – children simply love the rhythmic appeal of music and can't help but react to it.

A toddler loves to dance whenever she hears music and even a baby in arms giggles delightedly when whirled around by her parents in time to a tune. Sadly, when a child reaches school age, she may become more self-conscious about dancing expressively to music.

Nonetheless, a young child gets most pleasure from having the freedom to move in response to the music however she sees fit. Never mind that her movements do not resemble any dance you've ever seen before, the important thing is that she's enjoying herself. This means that formal dance lessons, such as ballet, jazz or tap classes, are probably better suited to an older child. Stick to musical movement until your child is mature enough to deal with the formal steps and discipline of a dance class.

Give your child lots of access to as many different types of music as possible and see what she likes best. Some children respond particularly well to simple percussion or a drum beat and they don't need sophisticated music in order to move expressively.

> 'Without music, life would be a mistake.'
> Friedrich Nietzsche

early signs of musicality

Repeating or recognizing theme tunes from
the television

Knowing if the tune goes up or down in
a nursery rhyme

Clapping out a simple rhythm

Listening and dancing to music with
evident enjoyment

Showing an interest in music

Distinguishing between sounds, for example with
eyes closed, knowing the difference between
tapping a cup or a glass

Singing a song from start to finish

Why not play some music and ask your child to move to what she hears? You can also suggest that she pretends to be certain objects, such as a tree in the breeze or a kite soaring in the sky, or even a colour. Your child is not limited by the same inhibitions as an adult and you'll be surprised by just how vivid and communicative your child's movements can be.

Dance and music can have deeply therapeutic benefits as well as being fun. It can help a child to unlock inner pain and express turmoil, if she has been through a particularly traumatic experience.

Music

No child should be without music. It can open creativity, soothe or stimulate the mind and give a child the chance to make sounds in her own way. Whether it is with a simple set of home-made shakers filled with dried beans (see right) or an elaborate musical instrument, the opportunity to make music is very important to the young.

Irrespective of whether she grows up in a musical household or not, a toddler is usually drawn to bang a

Contact can be made with autistic children through music, and it is used as therapy for the emotionally disturbed.

spoon on an upturned bowl or to crash saucepan lids like cymbals. All of this is testimony to a child's love of 'music-making' and is to be encouraged. Don't allow the fact that you consider yourself to be unmusical to prevent your child from having a go.

Singing

Although music is important to a child, it cannot replace the sound of a parent singing. A baby's first attempts at song come from trying to imitate her parents and a toddler will sing her dolls to sleep with the lullabies she hears from you.

Traditional nursery rhymes are a good starting point but any song will do if you prefer something more contemporary. Try bouncing your baby on your knee in

How to make a shaker rattle

YOU WILL NEED
A plastic bottle (any size)
Dried peas, beans or lentils
Superglue

METHOD
1 Clean out the bottle and allow it to dry thoroughly.

2 Fill the bottle to about a quarter of the way up with the peas, beans or lentils.

3 Carefully place superglue around the bottle opening and quickly tighten the lid. Allow the glue to dry completely before giving the shaker to your child to play with.

She may like to decorate the shaker herself with coloured paper, stickers or glitter.

accompaniment to nursery rhymes, and introduce your toddler to action songs, such as ring-a-roses or incy-wincy spider, and watch her delight.

A child under the age of seven learns best when she relates physically and emotionally to the material. So singing ditties to remember dates in history, or musically chanting the times table, is not as daft or draconian as it might at first seem. Vocalizing is an active way of learning and it can help to build a child's auditory memory.

Creative Play

If you forget all the playgroup activities, tumble-tot groups and sophisticated toys with which we bombard our children, you'll find that your child can entertain himself with the most basic of items through imagination and creative play.

It would be foolhardy to advocate that you abandon organized activities and toys completely, but why not consciously try to build in time for your child to amuse himself? You'll be surprised how much he can learn in this way.

Play is the cornerstone of a child's development. It is not something that a parent has to teach. Play and curiosity are instinctive and, while to see a child absorbed in play brings a smile to any parent's face, they also have an important role to fulfil.

Initially, it is through play that babies and toddlers explore and start to make sense of the world. Their senses are stimulated and they learn how to interpret every new sensation and experience, largely through creative play.

When your child gets to around the two and a half to three year old mark, he starts to become aware of his conscious self. He may use the 'I' form instead of referring to himself by his name and he is aware of his own identity. It is no coincidence then that, at around this age, he also starts to experiment with imaginary play (see page 100).

Fantasy Play

At this stage, there is no need for you to push learning on your child. He is quite happily exploring his fantasy world and, through it, intellectual growth is achieved without any conscious effort.

Fantasy play can help a child to transform the world into something less frightening. It helps him to recreate reality on a smaller and more manageable scale. It also assists him in practising the skills that he has acquired, to gain confidence and to take pleasure in his proficiency.

As a parent, your role is to provide equipment, materials and a suitable environment to feed his

> 'Play must ... not be left to chance, for it is through play that the child learns and learns eagerly and with enjoyment.'
> Friedrich Froebel, early 1800s

imitation

Since a young child learns instinctively through imitation, it is important to involve him in your activities as much as possible. Be warned, though. He cannot be fobbed off with pretend tools. He wants the real thing, or at least, scaled-down versions. So provide him with these and, when you're washing the car, digging the garden or preparing vegetables for dinner, don't be surprised if he wants to help. Of course, it will try your patience when his efforts are more of a hindrance but, if you can, let him join in and let him do it his way. This is how he starts to become part of the real world.

greenfile

Inuit children learn the strategies of hunting to feed the family by imitating their parents' skills through play from a very early age.

creative and imaginative powers. However, make sure the materials and the environments you expose him to are age-related. After all, top-quality parchment paper is somewhat wasted on a toddler's scribblings.

It is also important to provide opportunities for your child to make things, because the creative process produces enormous satisfaction. Depending on his preferences, he can have wonderful fun with paper, cardboard and glue, modelling dough, paints and crayons. Even tunnelling and digging on the beach is all grist to the creative mill – and it doesn't much matter that his sandcastle doesn't in the least resemble a classic turreted fortress. What's important is that it represents a castle to him. If you impose your values on his creativity, it will undermine him. By trying to

help or improve on his efforts, your child will get the impression that his version is inferior in some way. By all means show him a variety of processes from which he can choose, but let him develop them in his own way.

Time and Space

Children need new experiences in their lives to feed their creativity but they also need peace and time in which to assimilate what they've learned. It's good to provide them with opportunities to discover new things, but don't heap one on top of another at such a great rate that your child becomes blasé to them.

It is also helpful for a child to have his own space in which to play freely. Physically, this may mean a separate playroom or bedroom or a designated corner of a family room. However, it also means 'inner space', so that he does not feel crowded or rushed in his play.

Exponents of creative play believe that, if children are not allowed to give their imagination free rein, they can be emotionally damaged and their learning ability impaired. Educationalists stress the importance of allowing creative play to precede abstract thinking, but after the age of about four, you can introduce games that bring in concepts of time and space.

Jean Piaget, an eminent Swiss psychologist, established a connection between play and cognitive skills and development. He discovered that only after a child has gone through the intuitive thought stage is he ready to translate concrete experience into abstract thought and conventional learning.

Imaginary Play

A child needs the simplest of things to give scope to his imagination. Cardboard boxes can become anything from a den to a space rocket. Everyday things that come to hand are often seized upon, so a colander becomes a helmet, a stick becomes a sword and a teddy-bear can be a baby.

Some people believe that providing young children with 'perfect' toys robs them of their creativity because there is nothing for their imagination to work on. However, in my experience, it takes more than this to thwart a child's imagination. My sons simply used the 'perfect' toy for a completely different purpose from that for which it was designed.

Home-made Toys

The recyclable material that every household collects is a treasure trove for most youngsters. Cardboard and plastic packaging can be turned into a whole range of toys from dinosaurs to rockets and boats. And a toy that is the product of a child's imagination, and made by him (perhaps with a little help from you), carries additional meaning in his games.

Modifications and additions to bought toys may at first seem like wilful destruction but, for your child, it can add immeasurably to a toy's play value. So a wooden train and track becomes more enjoyable when the trucks are loaded with pebbles from the garden. A shop-bought dinosaur may make a better foe when embellished with armour made from colourful recyclable plastic packaging.

props to encourage creative and imaginary play

Water – sink, bowl, paddling pool, puddles, streams, bath. Add toys, sieves and bottles for endless possibilities.

Modelling dough, clay, mud pies.

Beads and pasta tubes for threading.

Paper, paint and colouring tools – pastels, chalks, felt-tipped pens, crayons – plus leaves and vegetables for blob-and-fold and printing (most kids also love to take their hand prints).

Old clothes, hats, masks for dressing up.

Nursery rhymes – rhythmic games such as pat-a-cake, round-and-round-the-garden and ring-a-roses, inspire babies and toddlers.

Musical instruments – home-made rattles, shakers, bells and drums.

Pretend tea-sets.

Dressing Up

Your toddler will love putting himself in someone else's shoes, whether it's an authority figure from the world he knows, such as a teacher or the postman, or whether it's a fictional character, such as Superman or Cinderella.

Your contribution to this imaginary land is the provision of a dressing-up box. Discarded clothes, old hats and shoes and the odd prop, such as a pair of sunglasses, form the backbone of a dressing-up box. Glittery evening attire is especially popular, and don't worry if there's some gender-bending cross-dressing going on – at this age, boys choosing high heels and spangly gowns is no indication of sexual proclivity in later life.

Hats, tiaras and masks are key props for make-believe games. The wearer is transformed into the new persona immediately. Add a few more props, such as an old saucepan and wooden spoon for setting up home games, or a chalkboard for playing schools, and hey presto, you've provided the finishing flourish to your child's dramatic play.

Making a mask

1 Using an old cereal box, cut out a basic eye-mask.

2 Holding it against your child's face, carefully mark where the eye holes should be and cut them out with a small pair of scissors.

3 Let your child paint and decorate the mask to create the character he wants, using sequins, fabric scraps, braid and beads.

4 Staple any additional pieces, such as whiskers or feathers, to the cheek area of the mask.

5 Make a hole on either side of the mask and thread a piece of elastic through, the right length to fit your child's head. Secure the ends of the elastic with knots so it doesn't slip through the holes.

Storytelling

If someone said that you could enter a fantasy world with your child and enjoy adventures and mysteries to your heart's content, you'd pay good money for the chance, wouldn't you? Well, in fact, you don't have to part with your cash. Instead, suspend disbelief for a short while, and enter the realm of storytelling. The only things that can limit the adventures are your own imagination or a misplaced sense of self-consciousness. Whether you let your imagination run riot or prefer to follow a traditional fairy tale, storytelling is a wonderful way to share a magical experience with your child.

Cultural Heritage

In some cultures, the art of storytelling is hugely important. Oral accounts are not only used to entertain but also as an essential tool for keeping traditions, history and cultural inheritance alive from generation to generation.

In the developed world, the oral tradition has been replaced by books, written records, television and cinema. Yet many believe that storytelling can provide rich material for children's imaginations and for their play-acting.

In fact, Rudolf Steiner, the philosopher and educationalist (see page 75), insisted that teachers should tell stories to the children, rather than read them, in his kindergartens and schools. He believed ardently in the need to create a vital connection between the teacher and the class and he thought this to be impossible if the teacher had her nose in a book. At Steiner schools, fairy tales, myths and legends are used extensively with the younger children as a prelude to history lessons when the child is older.

'If you want your children to be brilliant, tell them fairy tales. If you want them to be very brilliant, tell them more fairy tales.'
Albert Einstein

Fairy Tales

While most of us are more than happy to cuddle up with our youngsters and to read a book together, many parents balk at the idea of telling a tale without the prompt of the written word in front of them. If you're slightly embarrassed by the thought of spinning a yarn, start by recounting a story that is familiar to you. It doesn't matter if you tell Little Red Riding Hood every night for a week. In fact, repeating the story regularly, without changing the words, gives a young child a comforting rhyme and rhythm that is hugely reassuring in a potentially frightening world.

Then, as you grow in confidence, you can extend your repertoire, embellishing the details of the stories to suit yourself and your child, and immersing yourself in the wonder of the narrative. Bone up on a few of your old favourite fairy tales, share them with your child and just watch the expression on her face – it's truly magical.

Make-believe Tales

Once you've mastered reciting fairy tales, fables and legends, why not invent a story of your own? Little ones enjoy a thinly disguised account of what they have been doing, and can easily be drawn into the plot by asking questions such as, 'And what do you think happened next?'

A make-believe story can also be a very useful tool for persuading a pre-school child to think about or talk about difficult issues affecting them, particularly if you use a main character of roughly the same age as your child, who goes through a similar set of circumstances. Through invented tales, she might see how she can handle a situation or realize that she's not the cause of a problem, for example.

Storytelling can also be a good way of communicating difficult concepts, such as loss, separation and death, although if you have any doubts about your ability to invent a helpful story, there are books available that deal very successfully, and sometimes obliquely, with these topics.

If you're struggling to come up with ideas for a story, throw it open and let your child suggest a topic.

listening books

Audio tapes can be a marvellous way to share stories with your toddler. She'll love it when you listen, and even join in, together. Bear in mind, though, that a young child is easily distracted and may become disruptive if you expect her to pay attention to Harry Potter along with her older siblings. So stick to nursery tapes until she's older.

Children love to be involved and it will set you a challenge. Snuggle up, set the atmosphere and away you go. Another source of inspiration can be to choose an ornament or mystery object from around the house and weave a story around it. Let her hold the object while you recount the story and it will come to life in front of her very eyes.

The Right Tone

You'll know better than anyone what sort of stories will hold your child's imagination, but be reasonably sensible about the subject matter. A three-year-old could be scared witless by some of the more macabre fairy tales whereas a seven-year-old will find the same story gruesomely captivating. You'll tend to find that up to about the age of four, children take a story at face value. Five- to seven-year-olds, on the other hand, are able to analyze and consider a story, and they are able to understand quite complex ideas and plots. Whatever the age, storytelling should excite and entice your child's curiosity and, particularly when she's older, invite her to think more deeply about situations.

developing a child's moral sense

Being told fables, fairy tales and made-up stories can help a child:

• put himself in somebody else's shoes

• understand another's emotions and reactions

• reflect on how he feels and what he knows

• examine actions and consequences

• explore moral dilemmas

• challenge his own views from one step removed, if personal experience is too close for examination

A fairy tale usually starts with the phrase, 'Once upon a time …' and the opening scene is set in a perfect world. Then some form of obstacle arises, or a difficult trial takes place. Finally, good triumphs over evil and they all live happily ever after. Well, this is true for the character who successfully completes the challenge or quest, at least, because that one emerges a wiser and happier person for the ordeal, while the baddy is defeated and condemned.

In the past, this simplistic formula has drawn criticism from sceptics, who dismiss fairy tales as superficial, escapist and one-dimensional. Of course, in real life the good often suffer and the wicked may prosper, but fairy tales are not about realism.

Proponents of the traditional fairy tale believe that, quite apart from the fact that children love them, a child also recognizes a deeper wisdom in the story that can help to illuminate some of life's secrets for her.

Why not make up your own fairytales, with once upon a time and the classic happy-ever-after-ending?

Creative Art

Just as a child's speech is an indicator of what stage he's reached in his development, so his drawings or paintings can give you a similar idea, because art, like language, follows a particular pattern.

We tend to associate scribbling with a toddler but that is because this is the age at which most children are first given crayons. If, for some strange reason, your child did not have access to pencils and paper until he was six, he would start with exactly the same scribbles as a toddler before progressing to the more rhythmic and smooth shapes of an older child's drawing.

Irrespective of the culture in which children grow up, they all go through the same drawing stages. First come the dense circular or linear scribbles on the page. Then the lines become a little more controlled. From there, a child may progress to drawing circles within circles, or a circle with a cross or mark within it. This usually happens at about three years old and shows that the child is becoming aware of himself as a separate entity. As your child begins to explore the world, so this will be reflected in his art as he starts to draw shapes with lines radiating outwards.

Drawings of people start simply as a head, possibly with straight lines coming off it for arms and legs. Eventually, a trunk will appear, followed by feet and hands. By about five years old, he will start to make more realistic representations of objects, animals and people. At six, items are starting to be shown in some sort of scale and as they relate to others, e.g. sky at the top, house at the bottom with smaller flowers and trees in the garden. The seven-year-old is looking at things more closely and he wants to get detail into his art.

As parents, we should be aware that this pattern is pretty universal and resist trying to hasten the process along. Obviously, the child who loves to draw will, with lots of practice, progress through the stages quicker than a child who rarely picks up a crayon. However, as long as you are providing the resources and opportunities, the pace should be dictated by your child's preferences. It's not a race.

Equipment

Chubby crayons are the easiest option for little hands, and your child will soon progress to coloured pencils and felt-tipped pens. However, while toddlers are perfectly happy using these to scribble on a piece of scrap paper, remember that all children love to paint. This is a messy business, however restrained your child may be, and some preparation is needed to limit the potential damage to clothes, furniture and flooring. It may seem like an awful lot of effort to get out the paints – and then clean up – for a relatively short period of pleasure (they all get bored sooner than you'd like), but steel yourself and let him paint whenever possible, because his paintings can tell you a lot about how he's feeling.

Make life easier for yourself by buying ready mixed paints, having a painting overall and newspaper to cover surfaces. It makes the process less fraught for you and more relaxed and enjoyable for your child.

Art does not have to be limited to pencils, paint and paper. Craft shops offer a huge array of stencils, sponges and coloured papers and card as well as paints and pastels. The choice is boundless but these are for later, so don't let your enthusiasm get the better of you. Match the materials and equipment to the age of your child and the glitzy stuff can wait.

greenfile
Why not collect smooth rocks and stones with your toddler and let him have fun painting these, rather than using paper?

potato prints

Making prints with a baking potato and poster
paint – what could be simpler or more fun?

Energy Burning

According to the UK National Audit Office, nearly one-third of children between the age of two and fifteen are overweight or obese. With today's sedentary lifestyles, more children than ever before are at risk of becoming overweight and suffering from the inherent health and emotional problems that entails.

The good news is that the natural inclination of the vast majority of children is to be active, and kids burn a lot of calories just doing the job of growing up, so they have the edge over adults when it comes to weight management.

As a parent, your task is to take advantage of your child's natural exuberance and desire to be active, and to instil in her from the youngest age a love of exercise and healthy eating.

Motivation

For pre-school infants, the simple truth is that the best inspiration is their parents. Researchers now know that children who see their parents, particularly their mother, being active are among the most physically active themselves.

This doesn't mean you have to spend your leisure time playing exhibition tennis in front of your child. It is more an attitude of mind, and an approach to life that involves building activity into daily routines – taking the stairs rather than the lift, walking the dog, raking leaves. At weekends, why not arrange a picnic with another family and take a ball? How about wave jumping at the beach, hoisting her high as the waves rush towards the shore?

You might like to think about putting some age-appropriate items in the garden that will make being outside fun and tempting, such as a ball pool,

Experts recommend that children under two should not be allowed to watch any TV or DVDs. Over two years old, a child should watch no more than one or two hours a day and that includes time spent on computer or video games. US researchers suggest that obesity risks could be cut by around one-third if the average TV viewing time decreased from three hours a day to one hour a day.

an inexpensive sandpit or paddling pool (this will obviously need supervising). Chalk a hopscotch pattern on the patio – it will keep your three-year-old occupied for ages. A swing, small slide, seesaw, mini-climbing frame and mini-soccer nets are other popular items for the garden.

Your toddler will quite happily join in games with other children if you're prepared to be the leader and organizer. Ideas to get her pulse racing may include:

Follow my leader: Make it as energetic or gentle as you like. Just make sure you keep the kids on the move as you skip, hop, star-jump and dance around the garden or park.

Wacky races: You can organize egg and spoon races, sack races, three-legged races, walking backwards races. The list is endless and provides hours of fun. Although your three-year-old may not be old enough to join in all of them, she will love to watch with you and may play her own jumping up and down game at the same time.

Play-acting: You tell the story and the children act it out. You can make your imaginary tales as adventurous and wild as you like – small kids love pretending to be animals, superheroes and monsters.

Organized Activities

Baby swim sessions at your local pool are a good start. Staff play nursery tunes and encourage mothers to go for a supervised dip with their babies. Similar sessions are often offered for mothers and toddlers, for which most pools provide inflatable toys and colourful floats.

Toddlers can get a great deal of pleasure from organized gym sessions, which they attend with a parent. Often located in church halls or sports halls, Kindergym and Tumble Tots typically offer small climbing obstacles and floor equipment. The sessions, which are supervised by a trained leader, usually culminate in a group sing-song or a game with a soft, billowing parachute canopy, for example.

Although many children enjoy organized activity, this should not totally replace free play. Moreover, it is not recommended that a child starts competitive sports before the age of seven or eight. Before that age, most children do not have the necessary skills, the attention span or the concentration required to take part.

Bad-weather Activities

Bad weather does not have to preclude all activity for your youngster. If it is too bad, there are lots of indoor soft play areas where your child can kick off her shoes, launch herself into the ball-pit and burn off some excess energy. But as the comedian Billy Connolly says, 'There's no such thing as bad weather, just the wrong clothing.' So if it's not too rainy, gusty or snowy, wrap up your child in suitable attire and take her to the park. She'll probably love splashing in puddles in her wellies, flying a kite or making angels in the snow.

Health and Healing

The one thing parents wish above all else for their children is good health, and since health is so important to us, why are we happy to give our children drugs when very often a natural remedy will do the trick?

Natural medicine is gentle and effective, allowing children's bodies to deal with illness in the way that nature intended. It simply gives nature a helping hand, working in conjunction with the body.

Many of the treatments for common childhood ailments are things that our grandparents used and their grandparents before them. In fact, according to the World Health Organization, virtually 80 per cent of the world's population still rely on natural healing as their first form of healthcare. It is only in the so-called developed world that we rely on pharmacology and drugs to heal even the most common-place conditions.

An integrated approach to illness is probably the most sensible. Of course you can still take your children to the doctor – and should in many acute cases – but very often, you can successfully help and heal common childhood ailments using tried-and-tested natural medicines. The treatments suggested in this chapter are a great starting point.

NOTE:
The advice in this chapter is not to be considered as a substitute for medical advice from your family doctor or any other qualified medical practitioner. If you treat your child with natural medicines, such as herbs, you should always inform your doctor, because these can be very powerful and can interact with prescribed and over-the-counter medications.

Baby Health

When your baby first arrives, it's completely natural to worry about the smallest health niggles and to seek reassurance from health professionals on every occasion. As you grow in confidence, so you become better at judging what requires attention and what can be handled safely and sensibly by you at home. In my experience, if you are at all unsure, you should have your baby checked by your health visitor, GP or complementary health practitioner.

However, for colic, nappy rash and cradle cap, the tried-and-tested remedies used by our grandmothers have given excellent results over the years and continue to serve babies extremely well.

Colic

This condition is characterized by regular bouts of crying, which tend to occur at the same time(s) each day – usually in the early evening. Colic is most common in the first three weeks to six months of your baby's life and, after this, symptoms tend to mysteriously disappear.

During an attack, your baby is almost inconsolable and the whole experience can be extremely upsetting and draining for you. The signs of colic are:

• Crying, often accompanied by your baby drawing up her legs in pain
• Grumbling noises from her abdomen with plenty of burping and passing of wind
• Feeding, which consoles her temporarily but then appears to aggravate the situation.

If your baby seems to be crying incessantly, talk to your health visitor or go to see your GP to check that no underlying physical problem is causing the situation. Once your mind has been put at rest about that, try following these age-old remedies.

What to do
Gently massage her abdomen.
Give her a dummy to suck.
Rock your baby.
Lay your baby over your knee chest down and rhythmically rub her back.
Alternatively, stand or walk holding your baby along your forearm, chest down with legs either side of the arm and head in the palm of your hand.

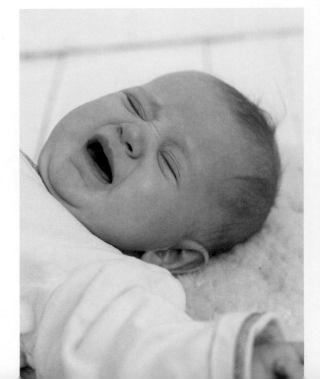

Take her for a ride in the car.

Burp her against your shoulder by gently patting or rubbing her back.

Offer small amounts of weak camomile, fennel or lemon balm tea. Breast-feeding mothers can drink these soothing herbal teas, which will pass through to the baby in the breast milk.

Be careful about your diet if you are breast-feeding. The worst foods for aggravating colic are grapes, peaches, plums, strawberries and pineapple; spicy foods, such as curries; garlic, onions, broccoli, cabbage, cauliflower, Brussels sprouts and pulses; alcohol; coffee and chocolate.

WARNING Don't automatically assume that irate crying during the evening is due to colic – check for other causes.

be kind to yourself

No matter how much you love her, having a baby who cries furiously and inconsolably every day is extremely draining and can strain the nerves of the most loving and laid-back parents. If you find yourself becoming demoralized and/or stressed by the daily screaming sessions, give yourself a break. The following suggestions are for you:

Wrap her up and get out of the house for a walk or a drive.

Get help. Don't try to cope on your own. Get your mother, mother-in-law or a friend to take the baby for an hour or so, giving you the opportunity to do something else and get away from the cycle of increasing tension. If you're not listening to constant whinging and crying, even if it's only for an hour, you will come back with more energy to cope with it.

Seek advice. Telephone your health visitor, GP or a parenting helpline (see Useful Contacts, page 156).

If you feel you cannot take any more, put your baby down gently in the cot and go into another room for a short while. Your baby is safer crying in her cot than in your hands at that moment.

Don't feel guilty. Just because your baby cries more than most other babies seem to do does not mean you are a bad parent – it's a matter of temperament, and also, unfortunately, the luck of the draw. Remember, your baby is not announcing to the world 'inadequate parenting' and this phase will pass in time.

Talk to other parents. Find out what helped others in a similar situation but remember to trust your instincts, because they rarely let you down.

Nappy Rash

This is caused by ammonia in the urine and digestive juices from the faeces irritating the skin in the nappy area, resulting in a red and occasionally spotty rash. While your baby is in nappies, there's every chance that she will get nappy rash at some point. Although common, with the right approach, this uncomfortable condition can be cleared up within a couple of days.

What to do

Allow your baby to spend as much time as possible without her nappy on.

Terry cotton nappies are less likely to trigger nappy rash than disposables – consider using cloth nappies, if only temporarily.

Change nappies frequently and make sure the nappy area is thoroughly cleaned each time.

If breast-feeding, beware of what you eat. Certain foods can be passed on to your baby, resulting in nappy rash. Citrus fruits, sugar, caffeine and some

greenfile

A scheme to recycle thousands of tonnes of used disposable nappies was launched in the UK in February 2009. The first of four plants, based in Birmingham, will be able to process 36,000 tonnes a year, with plastic recovered from the nappies used initially to make roof tiles. Other items, including cycling helmets, shoe insoles and cladding, could be made later. In a second phase, planned to be running by the end of 2011, methane will be extracted from the used nappies and sold to the national gas grid. Plants such as this already exist in Canada and the Netherlands and it's hoped the UK nappy recycling sites will reduce the quantity of material being sent to landfill by 4 per cent. For green parents who feel bad about using disposable nappies, this development could go part of the way to assuaging the guilt.

yeasted breads are often culprits. Dilute the effects of your diet by drinking plenty of water.

Treat the rash with an arnica or calendula cream and powder.

Use a zinc oxide barrier cream to protect the area. Apply it liberally and do not rub it in. This is particularly beneficial if used in conjunction with arnica or calendula cream.

Occasionally, nappy rash is caused by the fungal infection Candida (thrush), in which case, an infant dosage of a probiotic supplement in powder form may be helpful. Seek advice from your health visitor, complementary health practitioner or doctor.

greenfile

Floral waters that are safe for use with infants are both disinfecting and soothing for bathing your baby's nappy area. They have the same properties as essential oils but are gentler and do not need diluting.

Your baby has two soft spots on her skull, which are known as fontanelles. The smaller posterior fontanelle at the back of the head is triangular in shape and closes at around six weeks. The larger anterior fontanelle on the top of your baby's head, which is easier to feel, is diamond or kite shaped and this tends to stay open until well after your baby's first birthday, often until she's around eighteen months old. Keep an eye on your baby's soft spots because these can be a clue to the state of her health. For example, a sunken fontanelle can be a sign of dehydration.

Cradle Cap

Babies with the characteristic thick, waxy, yellowish crust on their head and, occasionally, on the eyebrows, eyelids, ears and nose, are suffering from seborrhoeic dermatitis, more commonly known as cradle cap.

This is caused by an over-production of sebum (natural oils) from the scalp. As the sebum dries, so it clogs the ducts of the glands, causing still more sebum to be produced. Although the condition looks unsightly, it should not cause your baby any discomfort and the crust is not itchy.

What to do

Wash the hair and scalp with a mild baby shampoo about three times a week to speed up the natural healing process.

Brush the hair and scalp with a soft bristle brush to encourage faster flaking.

Gently massage the scalp.

Mix one teaspoon of lemon juice with two tablespoons of olive oil and apply twice daily to the scalp. This can be left on, or rinsed off with warm water or a mild baby shampoo.

WARNING Do not pick at the crust or loose flakes because this will result in bleeding, which could lead to secondary bacterial or fungal infections taking hold.

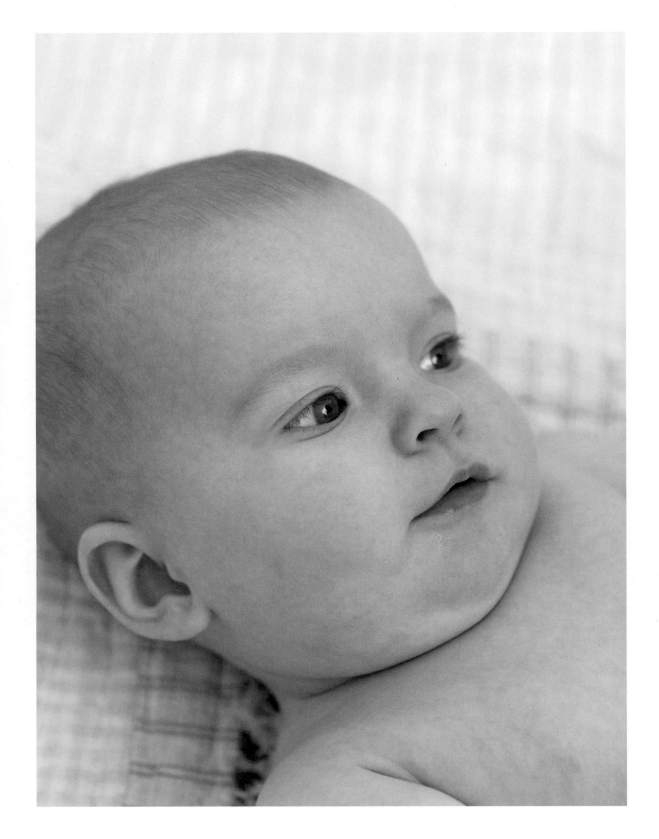

Common Complaints

There are a number of complaints that will almost certainly afflict your child at some point during her infancy – and for some unfortunate little ones they are a common occurrence. It's worth stocking up on a few basic natural ingredients that will help you to tackle diarrhoea, ear infections and fever when they strike.

Although the following treatments have been used to good effect for generations, if your child has recurrent bouts of any of these common complaints, take her to a health professional to check for underlying causes.

Diarrhoea

It is not unusual for young children to experience the odd bout of diarrhoea – not surprising either when you consider how they love to put things in their mouths. Diarrhoea is simply the body's way of eliminating a toxin or other harmful substance as quickly as possible.

Causes of diarrhoea include mild food poisoning, or a food that disagrees with her, bacteria and viruses, probably picked up from another child. Alternatively, when a child suffers from diarrhoea quite frequently, the underlying cause could be a food intolerance (have you introduced a new food recently?) or a digestive condition, such as coeliac disease, allergy or inflammatory bowel syndrome. If your child often suffers with diarrhoea, or if a bout of diarrhoea lasts longer than forty-eight hours and/or is accompanied by pain, pallor or unusual behaviour, consult a doctor.

In most cases, though, diarrhoea is the result of an infection or something ingested that doesn't agree with her. As a result, the intestinal tract becomes irritated and inflamed, so triggering its lining cells to produce more fluids. In turn, this increases the peristaltic action of the gut to eliminate the offending food or virus, which gives your child the characteristic stomach cramps and loose, watery stools associated with diarrhoea. Don't try to stem the diarrhoea, but take the following precautions.

What to do

Make sure your child remains hydrated. Offer water often and encourage her to sip rather than gulp down large volumes. Alternate water with a selection of diluted fruit juice, soup or broth.

If your child wants to eat, give her foods that absorb poisons and will not aggravate the gut any further, such as rice, pasta, bread and dry biscuits/crackers. Avoid protein and dairy produce (with the possible exception of live yoghurt – see below), because this will give the digestive tract a chance to recover. Similarly, refined sugars, caffeine and hard-to-digest fatty foods should be avoided or minimized as much as possible.

Sipping weak, cooled camomile tea can be calming and replenishing.

A child-friendly probiotic to encourage the replenishment of the bowel's natural flora can help. You can buy children's drinks containing probiotics, or give her live probifidus-containing yoghurt in small quantities.

greenfile

Your child's bottom can become extremely sore from regular wiping after a bout of diarrhoea. Washing and thoroughly drying the area and applying a little calendula cream can be very soothing.

Ear Infection

Some children's early years are blighted by frequent ear infections while for others they are a rarity. Nonetheless, most children will succumb to an ear infection of some sort by the time they are three years old, the most common one being otitis media. This infection of the middle ear is usually caused by bacteria or viruses, or by a common cold.

If you suspect your child has an ear infection – is he pulling at his ear and fractious? – consult your doctor, who will very likely prescribe antibiotics. In fact, antibiotics are effective only if a bacterial infection is confirmed. If it is viral, antibiotics are not the answer.

If your GP does not think the infection is bacterial, and agrees that waiting twenty-four hours or so before prescribing antibiotics is not a risk, some alternative treatments may be effective.

What to do

A couple of drops of warm olive, mullein or garlic oil in the ear every four hours can help.

Give your child echinacea drops at the appropriate dosage recommended on the packet.

Homeopathic remedies are often very effective. Consult a homeopath or a homeopathic manual for more detailed advice.

Keep the outer part of the ear clean and out of cold draughts.

Your child should be able to unblock his nose to equalize pressure in the ears. A health visitor will be able to advise you, or follow the instructions below.

greenfile

If you follow the conventional treatment of a course of antibiotics to treat your child's ear infections, remember to support his gut flora by giving him a good probiotic supplement and zinc, both available in specially formulated immune-boosting supplements for children.

Teaching your child to blow his nose

It may sound ridiculously simple to adults, but children often struggle with the concept of blowing their noses. At the toddler stage, you can help your child by showing him the technique in a fun way when he's well so that he's able to blow his nose when it's important, such as when he has an ear infection or cold.

Encourage him to feel the air coming from each of your nostrils, and then from his own.

Place a cotton-wool ball, or a strip of tissue screwed into a loose ball, on the table and get him to see if he can make it move using the air from his nose.

As he gets the hang of it, you could challenge him to a race.

Once he's used to blowing air from his nose, gently close one of his nostrils with your finger and encourage him to blow through one nostril. After several attempts, change to the other nostril.

Finally, hold a tissue over his nose at the outer edge of each nostril and ask him to blow into it.

Fever

Normal body temperature is about 37°C (98°F). Children frequently develop a raised temperature, usually due to viral infections that clear up of their own accord within a day. Occasionally, high fever can be a sign of a more serious illness. A persisting, recurrent or very high fever needs to be seen by a doctor.

That said, fever is not an illness in itself. It's a sign that the body is using its natural defence mechanism to fight an infection. So, from this perspective, a fever is a sign that the body is working as it is supposed to. A high temperature inhibits the reproduction of the bacteria or viruses that are causing the underlying illness, and also helps the body to excrete the resulting waste products and toxins.

Before you can treat a fever, you need to know what its cause might be. So, although natural healers usually recommend allowing a fever to run its course, you may want to bring down the fever so you can work out what's going on.

What to do

Keep your child in light cotton clothing if she is wet and clammy.

Sponge her face, neck and ankles with lukewarm water. Sponging the body can cause shivering and goose bumps, however, so stick to the face and the extremities.

Sweating and shivering can cause dehydration, so encourage your child to drink enough (her urine should be pale yellow – if it's darker, she may need to drink more).

Children rarely want to eat when they feel poorly,

---

taking your child's temperature

The best way to get an accurate temperature reading is to place a digital display thermometer in your child's armpit, directly against her skin, and hold the arm gently against her chest. The reading will be 0.5°C lower than if her temperature was taken with a thermometer in her mouth.

Aural thermometers, as used by most GPs – special thermometers with a cover over the tip that are placed carefully in the ear – are extremely accurate and are available to buy for home use but they are expensive.

Forehead thermometers and strips, which you hold against your child's forehead to get a reading, are not very accurate but can give a general idea of your child's temperature.

It's best to take your child's temperature as accurately as possible before considering giving any fever-reducing medicines.

---

so don't force her. Fluids are more important at this stage.

If you decide to give your child medicine to reduce a temperature, give only those that are suitable for her age group, such as children's paracetamol (e.g. Calpol) or ibuprofen (e.g. Nurofen for kids) and always follow the guidelines on the container. Never give aspirin to a child under sixteen years old.

WARNING A sudden increase in body temperature in young children can occasionally lead to febrile convulsions (fits). During such a seizure, your child may shake and twitch and the eyes may roll back in her head. Although extremely frightening, a convulsion usually lasts less than fifteen minutes and your child should make a full recovery within an hour. In most cases, a fit does not represent a serious condition but all fits should be reported and your child should be examined by a doctor immediately.

---

greenfile

Some immunizations can result in fever, so keep a close eye on your child at this time.

The Immune System

Much as we'd all love to be able to protect our children from illness, wrapping them in cotton wool and keeping them away from other children ultimately does them a great disservice.

Allowing them to mix with other children and to be among the population generally is great for their socialization, and it also means that they will inevitably come into contact with viruses and illnesses that will challenge and build their immune systems.

The following common illnesses – coughs and colds, chicken pox and mumps – can be treated naturally to great effect although, in many cases, it is not a case of curing the illness but of alleviating your child's symptoms in the most natural way possible.

Coughs and Colds

A baby is largely protected from coughs and colds during her first few months thanks to her mother's antibodies. After this, children build up their own resistance as they come into contact with other people. Naturally, as they get to nursery or playgroup age, or if they have an older school-aged sibling, they are exposed to far more infections and so are likely to have frequent coughs and colds.

Your child will usually recover without requiring any medical treatment within a few days, but the following remedies may alleviate symptoms while she's suffering. If symptoms persist or your child is particularly unwell, consult a doctor.

Remember, although a cough sounds bad, it is the body's way of eliminating foreign substances from the respiratory passages.

Treating a cough

First and foremost, you have to identify which type of cough your child has, since each requires a different approach. Does the cough get worse at night? This is often a sign of inflammation that is aggravated when your child lies down. A dry cough may be due to a nose, ear or throat infection, or a precursor to croup, while a wet, loose cough could be a sign of bronchitis or even a symptom of an allergic reaction, so be vigilant. The following natural approaches can help to ease cough symptoms.

What to do for a cough with phlegm

Avoid mucus-forming foods, such as dairy products, and anything sugary for a while.

An elderflower tincture, tea or cordial can be beneficial.

Sitting with your child in a humid atmosphere can relieve congested airways – boil an electric kettle with the lid off for a few minutes in your child's nursery, or run a hot bath with the bathroom door shut.

Gently rub her chest and throat with a mild, natural, eucalyptus-containing rub.

What to do for a dry cough

Again, sitting in a steamy room can help. Add a few drops of liquorice or linseed oil to the hot water for more effective steam inhalation.

Giving her a cooled infusion of dried sundew herbs to sip after meals can help (1–2g dried herbs to a cup of boiling water).

---

old wives tale

It seems that the idea of chicken broth being able to alleviate a cold is actually based on scientific fact. The protein helps to thin the mucus and promote repair while the chicken cartilage is believed to have an antiviral effect.

---

taste. Allow the tea to cool before giving it to your child to sip. Inhaling the steam is also beneficial.

WARNING If your child starts coughing very suddenly, has difficulty in breathing, becomes red or even blue in the face, she may have inhaled a foreign object. Call an ambulance without delay.

Treating a cold

A cold is caused by a viral infection of the upper respiratory tract. The mucus membranes swell, resulting in difficulty breathing, so that mucus production increases, resulting in a blocked or runny nose. As well as these symptoms, others may include a cough, headache, sneezing, aching muscles and a slight fever. A cold can last anything from three to ten days and children tend to catch between six and nine colds per year compared with an adult's modest two.

What to do

Keep your child well hydrated – make sure she drinks twice as much as her normal daily intake.

Giving her echinacea drops as soon as the cold starts can help (follow the dosage on the packet).

There is some truth to the adage 'feed a cold and starve a fever' so indulge her food fancies, providing they're not too unhealthy.

Ginger tea is great for warming the body and relieving cold symptoms. Chop 12mm of fresh root ginger and put it in hot water. Add honey for a sweeter

We have more colds in winter not because of the cold weather but because we spend more time together indoors, where viruses thrive in the moist, humid air, although exposure to cold and wet may lower your body's resistance to viruses.

Chicken Pox

Most children catch chicken pox at some stage during their pre- or early school years because it is such a prevalent and highly contagious childhood infection – and that's actually quite a good thing since its adult equivalent, shingles, is much more serious.

Chicken pox is caused by a herpes virus known as varicella-zoster. The first you might know about the infection is when your child is tired, off his food, complaining of a headache or has a slight fever. After a few days, the telltale flat, red spots appear on his body. These turn into blisters, which dry, crust over and disappear after twelve days or so. Remember, your child is contagious from at least two days before the first symptoms appear until all of the blisters have dried and scabbed over.

Orthodox medicine offers antihistamine-style creams to stop the itching but, over the years, many natural treatments to give children relief from this infernally itchy rash have come to light.

What to do

Using a sterile swab, dab the blisters with diluted lavender or bergamot oil before the scabs form to help the drying process.

Some mothers swear by swabbing spots with Manuka honey to promote healing.

A cool bath with up to ten tablespoons of sodium bicarbonate added can relieve itching.

Put 30g of dried mallow flowers and/or leaves to infuse in 1 litre of boiling water and leave for ten minutes. Once cooled, use to soothe affected areas several times a day.

Once the scabs have gone, use a good-quality rose oil to prevent scarring.

WARNING If in any doubt about the diagnosis, or if the rash is very severe, contact your doctor or complementary medical practitioner for advice.

A qualified complementary practitioner, such as a homeopath, herbalist or nutritionist, will be able to give advice on immune-boosting supplements and remedies to help your child's body deal with, and recover from, chicken pox.

greenfile

Ensure your child drinks plenty of water or liquids to prevent dehydration and keep the atmosphere in his bedroom humid and at a temperature of 18–20°C (64–68ºF).

Mumps

This is a viral infection that affects glands throughout the body but principally those under the jaw and in front of the ear.

Children spread the illness from one to another through coughs, sneezes and physical contact. Mumps usually lasts about ten days during which time your child is contagious. Early signs of the illness include a fever, headache, lack of appetite and aching muscles. These are followed by pain in the ear and jaw after which the characteristic swelling starts, resulting in the infamous hamster look. In fact, it's not very funny for the sufferer, and these swollen glands can be extremely painful. On the plus side, once your child has had mumps, he should have lifelong immunity.

Most UK children are vaccinated against mumps as part of the MMR vaccine programme, and a similar programme is offered in the USA.

What to do

Make sure your child has plenty of rest.

Keep him well hydrated.

Cool compresses applied to the swollen glands can give relief.

Swallowing is difficult and painful so avoid acidic foods, such as tomatoes, citrus fruits and orange juice.

Avoid highly flavoured foods that make the mouth water, so increasing pain.

Warm camomile tea can calm your child and help to reduce the fever.

WARNING It's rare for complications to arise but occasionally, especially in older individuals, the infection can affect the testes, brain or pancreas, with serious repercussions including long-term infertility.

greenfile

If your child turns up his nose at camomile tea, allow it to go cold and make ice lollies from it. He can suck these and still get the healing herbal benefits.

The Great Outdoors

As your baby becomes more mobile, one of the great pleasures of parenting is to spend time with her outdoors. Whether it's playing in a sandpit in the garden, day trips to the park and seaside, or more adventurous holidays, getting your child into the fresh air for some outside fun is a treat for you all. The downside is that inquisitive toddlers invariably end up with the odd scrape, tumble or bump, so check the 'green' first-aid advice on page 132. Also, be prepared with the relevant natural medical kit for insect bites and motion sickness, which are common problems for outdoor kids.

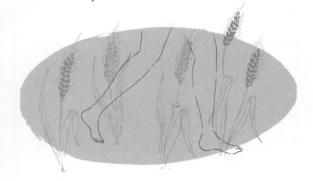

greenfile

Paradoxically, the most problematic bites are often those given by other children, since the human mouth carries many viruses and parasites that can cause infection. So if your child is bitten by another child or sibling and the bite breaks the skin, make sure you flush the area immediately with running water and then soak the injury in a saltwater solution (five tablespoons of salt per half litre of water) and then treat the affected area with an antiseptic cream. If the area becomes red or inflamed, consult a doctor.

Insect Bites

By far the best form of protection from insect bites is prevention, but keeping gnats, mosquitoes and other stinging insects out of a holiday room when toddlers are running in and out is no mean feat.

You can prevent most bites by dousing exposed skin with citronella, eucalyptus or lavender essential oils diluted in a carrier oil, such as almond. You can also burn citronella impregnated candles in the vicinity, although always keep them out of the reach of enquiring little fingers. For mosquitoes, natural repellents containing an Indian herb called neem have been proven to be very effective. However, if your child is bitten despite your best efforts, be prepared to alleviate the pain and itching with natural remedies.

What to do

Apply calendula or tea tree oil to relieve gnat and mosquito bites.

Arnica, calendula and/or hypericum or urtica creams can ease the itch of insect bites.

Cold or ice compresses applied as soon as possible can give relief, but don't let ice touch the skin directly.

WARNING Some of the powerful commercial insect repellents containing chemicals can be hazardous to babies and children. These should be avoided.

First Aid

Once your baby is on the move, he will probably receive his fair share of bumps, bruises, cuts and scrapes. It's all part of a toddler's need to explore combined with the fact that his body is not as coordinated as that of an adult.

Most incidents are minor and can be treated perfectly well at home with a large helping of TLC on the side. The following tips for home healing will prove invaluable as his enquiring mind leads him into numerous tricky situations.

Cuts and scrapes

A perennial problem for toddlers – you'll soon be adept at dealing with grazed knees and elbows!

What to do

Clean the wound with water and then dab with diluted tea tree oil (very weak) to disinfect.

If there is any debris, such as grit, left in the wound, pick it out gently with your fingers or carefully remove it with tweezers.

When the cleaned area is dry, gently apply a calendula-based cream.

WARNING A deep and gaping cut needs medical treatment and you should take your child to the A&E department of your local hospital or to your GP's surgery for attention. The wound may require stapling or stitching.

Bruises

It's rare to see a young child without a bruise somewhere on his arms or legs – not surprising when you think of how often toddlers take a tumble, or stumble into furniture. Most resulting bruises need nothing more than a quick rub and a 'kiss-it-better' at the time of the accident, but if a bruise is tender, swollen or sore, you can try the following natural treatments.

What to do

Arnica cream is wonderful – I never left home without it when my children were small.

Apply a cold compress or ice pack (wrapped in a clean cloth) to the site immediately.

A salt-water bath can ease bruising.

Add a couple of drops of lavender or hyssop essential oil to a ¼ cup of base oil and massage gently into large bruises.

WARNING Consult a doctor if you are concerned about any bruising, if you think it may be associated with a sprain or fracture, or if the swelling does not go down.

greenfile

Occasionally, a child who bruises easily may be deficient in vitamin C, vitamin K and/or bioflavonoids, all of which are involved in either the building of strong blood vessels or blood-clotting. A children's vitamin supplement containing these nutrients could be beneficial.

greenfile

Manuka honey comes from New Zealand bees that have collected pollen from the tea tree. It is a powerful natural antiseptic and has remarkable healing properties that are ideal for treatment of open wounds, such as minor cuts and scrapes.

Blisters

Even well-fitted shoes can cause blisters if your child wears them with no socks and/or wet feet.

What to do

Apply arnica or hypericum cream or lotion to the unbroken blister.

Consider using herbal remedies, such as arnica or urtica urens, which is a form of nettle, in the correct child dosage.

If the blister is open, wash the sore area with diluted tea tree oil and apply calendula cream or aloe vera gel.

greenfile

A blister occurs when there is friction, a pinch or excess heat, causing fluid to escape from damaged blood vessels. Since this fluid contains nutrients that can help to repair the damage, it should be left to do its job, so do not burst a blister.

Sprains and strains

Although it may seem as if our children are made of India rubber, an active toddler can sometimes overdo it or trip over and sprain a joint or strain a muscle. The most common sprains, which involve stretching the ligaments, are to ankle, fingers and toes, and are characterized by sharp pain at the moment of trauma, swelling of the joint, bruising and restricted mobility.

It's hard to differentiate between a mild sprain and a muscular strain but both are painful with swelling, and both limit movement.

Both sprains and strains must be allowed to heal fully. Otherwise they may become a recurrent problem in the future.

What to do

Apply a cold compress or ice pack (wrapped in a clean cloth) to the area for a maximum of 20 minutes at a time.

Restrict movement of the affected area. You can use a splint or bandage if you think it's necessary.

Give your child Arnica 6 remedy (at the dosage recommended on the packet) every ten minutes, and apply arnica-based gel or cream to the injury.

Don't give painkillers, except at night, because if it doesn't hurt, your child will want to move when the limb needs resting.

WARNING If movement is still painful after twelve hours, consult a doctor or take your child to the local hospital for an X-ray to establish if there is a fracture.

Making and applying a splint

Find something rigid to use as supports, such as boards, sticks, or even rolled-up newspapers. An injured finger or toe can be taped to the finger or toe next to it to keep it immobile.

Extend the splint beyond the injured area. In general, try to include the joints above and below the injury in the splint.

Secure the splint with tape above and below the injury. If you haven't got any tape, improvise using belts, ties or strips of clean tea towel or other cloth. Make sure the knots are not pressing on the injury and, in any case, be careful not to fix the splints too tightly, because this can cut off circulation.

Keep your child quiet and still and check the injured area frequently for swelling, numbness or paleness. If necessary, loosen the splint.

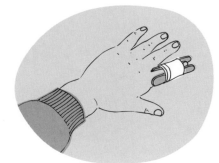

Motion Sickness

Long car journeys can be fraught when travelling with young children but the situation is made infinitely worse if your child suffers from motion sickness. This is not limited to car journeys, of course, and can affect susceptible individuals whether travelling by road, sea or air. Whatever the mode of transport, the symptoms are much the same – headache, pallor, dizziness, cold sweats and nausea, sometimes resulting in vomiting. All these are caused by the effects of movement on the delicate organs of balance in the inner ear. As your child gets older and his body becomes more used to travelling, so his brain recognizes the conflicting messages from the eyes and the balance centre in his ears, and the nausea usually diminishes.

What to do

Give your child a ginger tincture, either directly under the tongue or diluted in a cup of water, starting on the day before travel. Adjust the dosage of the tincture to his age group, according to the packet instructions.

Include fruits rich in antispasmodic flavonoids, such as bilberries and blackcurrants, in your child's diet in the days preceding travel.

Make sure you do not give your child a large meal before travelling – a full stomach can aggravate motion sickness.

Give your child a herbal travel sickness preparation about twenty minutes before setting off. Adjust the dosage to his age group, according to the packet instructions. If these over-the-counter preparations are available only in tablet form, consult a herbalist, homeopath or naturopath for a liquid or powder preparation for children.

Travelling in the front of the car rather than the back lessens movement, but see the section on car seats on page 50.

Encourage your child to look out of the window rather than drawing or looking at picture books. Put on an audio book to engage his attention.

Discourage him from leaning forward in his seat or closing his eyes. Although he may be restless, try to persuade him to sit still – putting a pillow behind his head to minimize head movement can help.

Make sure no strong food or unpleasant fume smells can affect him.

Open windows to allow fresh air into the car rather than using air conditioning.

greenfile

If your child suffers from motion sickness, travel well prepared with bowls and/or bags, wipes and water, and don't give up on travelling – it is very rare for a child not to grow out of motion sickness.

In the past, Chinese sailors used to chew on raw ginger root to prevent seasickness.

Natural Therapies

6

During pregnancy and early motherhood many women re-evaluate their approach to medicine, particularly since certain conventional medications cannot be taken at this time. An integrated approach, combining both conventional medicine and complementary therapies, often brings the best results.

The treatment you choose will depend on your symptoms and on your personal preferences. Complementary therapies can help you prepare for the birth, provide pain relief in labour, ease nursing difficulties and help your baby through her early months. Yet it brings peace of mind to know that modern obstetric and paediatric doctors are available should the need arise.

Many doctors and midwives are happy to work alongside complementary practitioners, and some are themselves trained in certain complementary skills. In this chapter, we look at a number of therapies, ranging from manipulative treatments that involve a hands-on approach, such as massage or chiropractic, to medicinal therapies that involve taking drops, tinctures or teas, such as homeopathy and herbalism.

Each therapy has its own governing body and it is essential that you check that practitioners are properly qualified, fully insured and covered by a code of ethics. For further details on a particular therapy or for a list of local practitioners, contact the individual association (see Useful Contacts, page 156).

Acupressure

Along with its better-known cousin acupuncture, acupressure is part of the comprehensive system of Traditional Chinese Medicine (TCM) that dates back thousands of years. Just like acupuncture, acupressure stimulates pressure points on the body to release muscular tension and promote the circulation of blood and the body's life force to aid healing. However, it is particularly suitable for babies and young children because, unlike acupuncture, no needles are involved and it is completely non-invasive. In fact, it is more akin to a firm massage.

The philosophy behind TCM is completely different from western medical thinking. According to Chinese belief, the key to health lies in the balance of two opposing forces (yin and yang, the passive and active force). Achieving balance and harmony is the fundamental objective of this complex and sophisticated system of medicine, which emphasizes the close interaction of mind and body.

Healthy balance relies on the smooth flow of vital energy known as qi (pronounced 'chee') through channels or meridians in the body. Imbalance or ill-health occurs when there are blockages or weaknesses in the flow of this energy, or if outside influences such as excessive heat, cold or damp are allowed to affect the body.

What to Expect at a Consultation
Treatment is preceded by very careful questioning and observation. When treating your child, a TCM practitioner will look at how she moves and take account of her size. If she is old enough, the practitioner will talk to her and listen carefully not only to what she says in response, but to how she says it, her tone and her attitude. The practitioner will inspect your child's tongue, and feel the six pulses on her wrists (three on each according to TCM) and take down details of her medical history, lifestyle, sleep patterns, eating habits, likes and dislikes, and so on.

From this, the practitioner will decide on a course of treatment, often using a combination of acupressure together with herbs.

Western acupressure practitioners who do not use other TCM techniques also require a case history before treatment. This is then followed by a 30- to 60-minute session where acupressure points on the body will be stimulated by firm finger or hand pressure.

acupuncture without needles

For those parents who favour acupuncture but are understandably anxious about having needles stuck in their child, there is now an alternative. Laser acupuncture is becoming more widely available for children, as is ultrasound acupuncture. Nothing breaks the skin – a small pen-like instrument is simply held on the spot and a low-dose laser beam stimulates the acupoint. Your child should not feel any discomfort at all.

benefits of acupuncture and acupressure

Pregnancy: Both acupressure and acupuncture are ideal for treating common pregnancy problems, such as morning sickness, nausea and backache. Either treatment is also effective against stress-related problems, pelvic pain, headaches, migraine, constipation, haemorrhoids, varicose veins and many conditions that you may have had prior to pregnancy for which you can no longer take medication.

You can expect to see improvement after six to ten treatments.

Labour: Acupressure points can be stimulated by a practitioner or as a self-help therapy (with some training) not only to encourage labour but to help dilate the cervix, to intensify contractions, for relaxation and for pain relief.

Acupuncture can also be used very effectively during labour for pain relief. For those women who want a totally natural birth, acupressure and/or acupuncture can be an ideal choice. Acupuncture can also be used to help the placenta deliver naturally without the need for an injection.

Post-natal mothers: Acupressure can help with post-natal joint pain and relaxation in particular.

Babies and toddlers: Acupressure can be used to treat many common problems experienced by babies and young children.

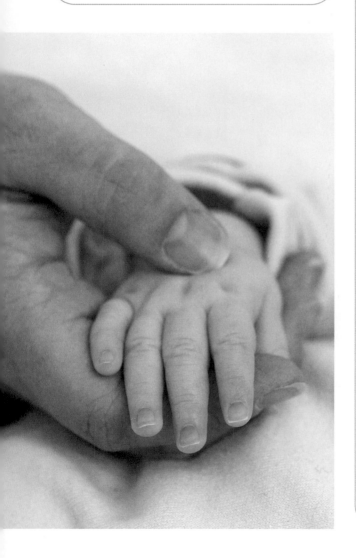

Chiropractic

This therapy involves manipulating the body's joints. It was developed at the end of the nineteenth century by Daniel David Palmer, who believed that if a vertebra is displaced, it may press against nerves and so cause an imbalance, resulting in discomfort, pain or even disease.

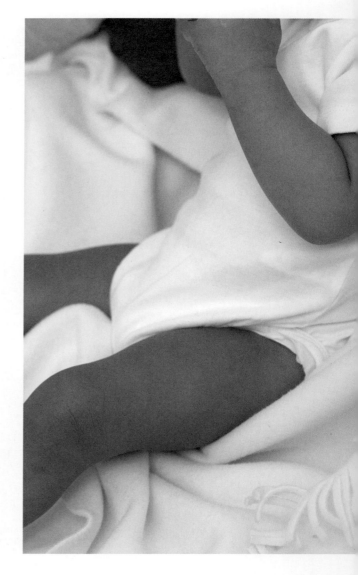

Chiropractic treatment uses gentle pressure and manipulation of the spine to relieve irritation on the nerves, which run through the centre of the spinal column. If the bones in your baby's spine are even slightly twisted during birth, this can cause several problems, such as unsettled sleep patterns, crying, poor feeding and a generally irritable baby.

Treatment is carried out by means of precise adjustments, in a similar way to osteopathy (see page 146). There are many similarities between the two therapies but one difference lies in the emphasis placed on soft tissue and spinal manipulation techniques. Chiropractors are also trained to take, and diagnose from, X-rays, but this is not applicable to babies.

In chiropractic, the emphasis is on alleviating existing problems and promoting long-term preventative health care. Many medical professionals accept the worth of chiropractic and, in the UK, some now agree that all babies should have their spines assessed shortly after birth, as they do in the USA. This is because the birth process can result in babies being born with slight damage to the spine – if the second stage of labour is long or difficult, for example, or if

greenfile

Danish research suggests that colic can originate from spinal-nerve stress and that chiropractic management is significantly more effective than medical treatment with colic drops.

benefits of chiropractic

Pregnancy: Physical and chemical changes in your body during pregnancy can aggravate spinal problems or make your back unstable, which is where a chiropractor can help. You may also find relief from lower back and pelvic pain in late pregnancy, and a chiropractor can advise on how to adapt your lifestyle in order to make daily routines easier. This is a drug-free treatment.

Post-natal mothers: This therapy is particularly effective in dealing with back problems associated with a difficult birth.

Babies and toddlers: Chiropractors have reported success in treating colic, breathing difficulties and sleep and feeding problems. As your child gets older, chiropractic treatment can be useful for asthma, hyperactivity, bedwetting and for dealing with physical problems after falls and tumbles.

induction results in a quick birth. Medical interventions, such as a caesarean birth or use of ventouse (a vacuum extractor) or forceps, can also contribute to spine damage. Although serious injuries are normally picked up at the time of delivery, minor problems can at first go unnoticed in a healthy baby.

What to Expect at a Consultation

The chiropractor will want to know about your baby's birth and medical history, and will examine your baby, feeling for any areas of muscular spasm and tenderness. Her joints may also be examined. A set of standard neurological and orthopaedic tests will be carried out. Chiropractors are trained to recognize any underlying conditions that need to be referred to

your GP or another specialist. A course of treatment for a baby usually involves four or five visits for newborns but may involve more sessions for toddlers and older children.

WARNING When looking for a chiropractor to treat your baby or child, it is best to find one who is skilled in paediatric care, which involves extra training.

Massage

'It is the most natural thing in the world for new parents to stroke, cuddle and rock their babies, and massage is no more than an extension of this desire to hold, touch and provide comfort,' says Clare Maxwell-Hudson, one of the world's foremost practitioners of massage.

Certainly, calm, soothing strokes can help to ease anxiety and minimize crying, and research has shown that massage can boost a baby's immune system, lower stress levels, relieve colic and encourage sleep.

More importantly, massage can be such a great pleasure and highly relaxing for you both. In this way, it can play an important role in helping you to bond with your baby, especially if you've struggled due to post-natal depression, or if you or your baby have experienced medical problems.

Fortunately, the benefits of massage for the very young have been recognized for some time and so you can generally find a baby massage class locally if you ask your health professionals or at the library.

Getting Started

There are very few babies who do not respond well to massage but, like adults, they all have different preferences and tolerances. You will discover what pleases your baby largely by trial and error and by being responsive to her reactions.

All babies feel the cold, so you'll get off to a better start if you always ensure that the room is warm throughout the massage and that your baby is comfortable. Massaging her on thick towels or cushions on the floor is one method. Having her on your lap is another option. Choose a location that makes you both feel comfortable and relaxed. Your baby will react to your calmness and the confidence of your touch – it should be a pleasure for you both.

The length of a massage depends entirely upon how long your baby enjoys it, but all the time she can see your attentive face and feel your caressing touch, you'll probably find that she is content. Singing or talking to her throughout is also recommended.

greenfile

Gentle stomach massage can help babies who are suffering from colic. By increasing circulation and stimulating peristalsis, it can help to relieve gas and constipation. After your baby is four weeks old, why not get into the habit of giving a brief tummy massage when changing nappies, or before a feed?

In a research study carried out at the Miami Medical Center in the USA, premature babies were given three fifteen-minute massages per day for ten days. They averaged a 47 per cent greater weight gain per day than the infants who were not massaged, and were more alert and active. The massaged babies were also in hospital for an average of six days less than the unmassaged group.

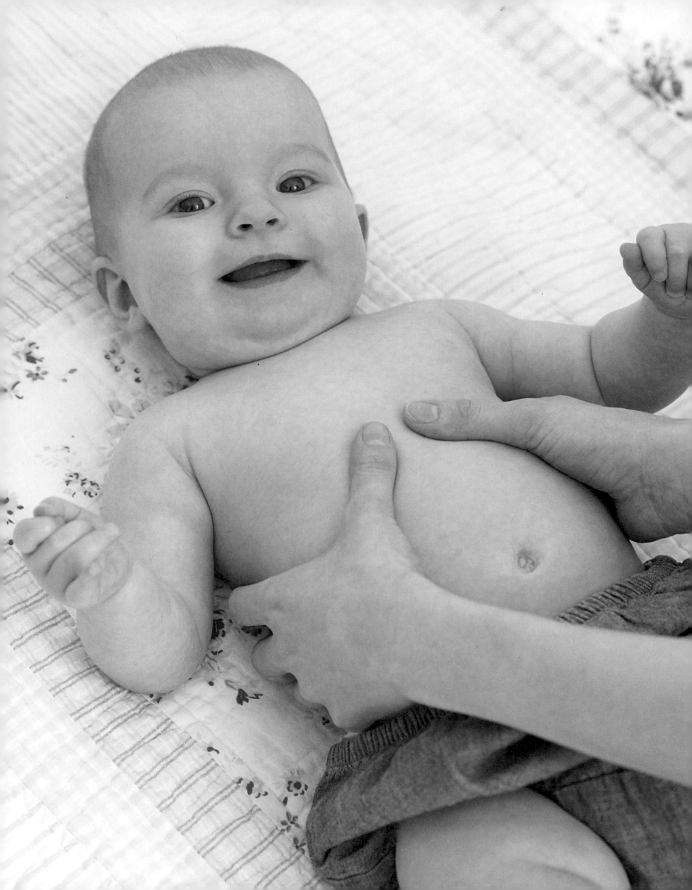

Relaxing massage

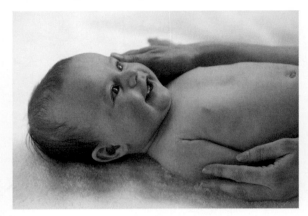

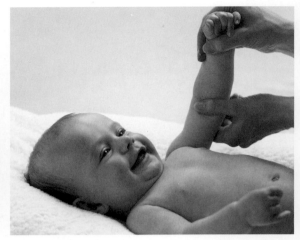

1 Start with your baby facing you and establish eye contact. Then focus your eyes on the area to be massaged before using your hands.

As you begin, warm a light, unscented oil (grapeseed is a good choice) or baby oil in your hands. It's recommended that you avoid aromatherapy and nut-based oils.

2 Gently start on your baby's upper arms, using your thumbs to caress the shoulders, and work down the arms to the hands, paying particular attention to the palms. Be careful near the elbows, which are particularly sensitive.

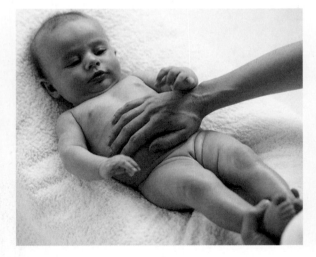

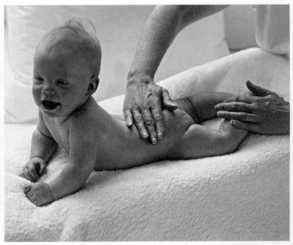

3 Then, using your finger tips, make circular motions from side to side across the chest, working down to the tummy (only massage her tummy after she is four weeks old).

4 Hold your baby's legs at the top and, using your thumbs, massage down from thigh to ankle. Also rub the soles of her feet with your thumbs.

5 As you and your baby grow in confidence, you will eventually be able to turn her onto her tummy and very gently massage down the back with your finger tips (avoiding the spine).

The session should take around ten minutes but if your baby starts to cry, stop and try again another day.

benefits of massage

Pregnancy: Many women experience the benefits of massage at this time, ranging from those who simply want to stay relaxed and healthy through pregnancy to those feeling the normal aches and pains. It is particularly helpful for backache and tired, swollen legs. A foot massage is excellent for aching feet in hot weather. Massage can also prevent stretch marks and is effective in calming and reassuring women who are frightened about the birth. Towards the end of the pregnancy, you can lie on your side or be supported to be massaged.

Labour: Massage therapists can attend a birth but often it is useful for a partner to learn some basic massage movements to help you through labour. 'Pain is more intense if you are tense or afraid. If the touch of massage can relax and reassure a mother, it's useful,' says Christine Westwood, who practises massage and meta-aromatherapy.

Post-natal mothers: Massage can help you to get your figure back after the birth. It's also a way to pamper yourself and to relax, which the baby notices and benefits from, too.

Babies and toddlers: Babies' limbs are very malleable so you must be gentle. However, simple stroking, which you probably do naturally, is the basis of massage. Adding oils comes next. Attending a baby massage group to learn how to do it may be useful. Most babies love massage but it is particularly beneficial for fractious, nervous or colicky babies.

WARNING Before trying out infant massage, be sure to learn about proper techniques. Many books and videos are available on the subject, and you could also check websites and contact your local hospital or baby class to find out if there are classes in infant massage in your area.

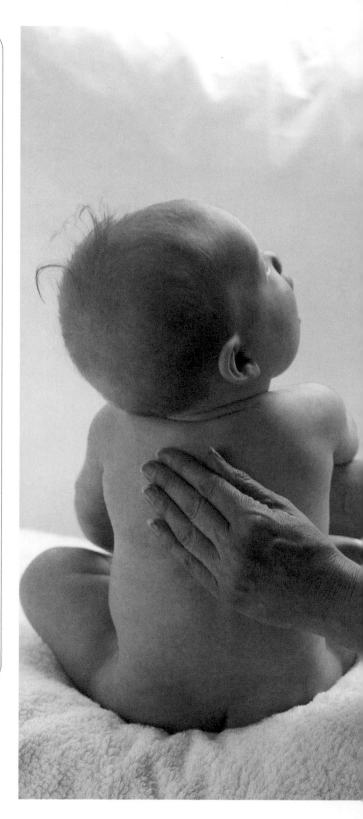

Osteopathy

Osteopathy focuses on the musculo-skeletal system – bones, joints, muscles, ligaments and connective tissue – and the way in which it works with the body as a whole. An osteopath will make adjustments by massage and manipulation, so that the body can heal itself. Within osteopathy, there are several specializations, including cranial osteopathy, which concentrates on the head. For this, very small movements and gentle manipulation are used, and so it is a popular treatment for babies and small children. Good results are reported with many childhood problems, ranging from colic to glue ear.

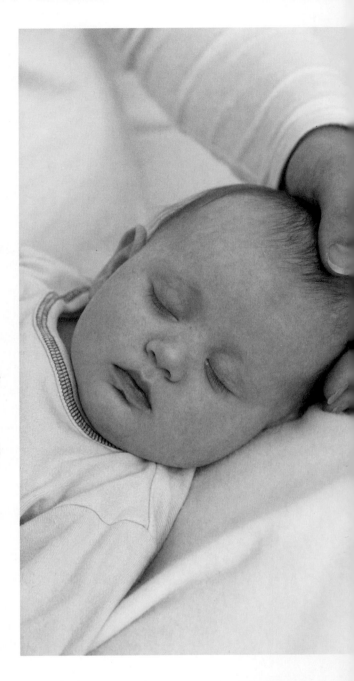

A paediatric osteopath trains for a further two years after achieving a general osteopathy degree. The practitioner uses very gentle manipulation of the body to bring about profound changes within the child's various body systems – the nervous system, the immune system, the muscular system and the circulatory system – to help them work more effectively than before. The treatment uses no drugs and is non-invasive. Paediatric osteopathy is used to treat children with conditions ranging from relatively minor ailments, such as glue ear, to asthma and epilepsy.

benefits of osteopathy

Pregnancy: Osteopathy is most commonly sought for any form of backache during pregnancy but it is also helpful for treating morning sickness, haemorrhoids, swollen legs and hands, and for moving the baby into a more comfortable position. Although osteopathy is safe throughout pregnancy, many osteopaths avoid giving treatment at the transition from the first to the second trimester (around twelve weeks) because this is a particularly vulnerable time.

Post-natal mothers: Treatment by an osteopath can help both mother and baby to get over the shock of the birth, and is available in some hospitals. Some specific after-birth problems, such as stress-incontinence or shoulder pain from breast-feeding, can benefit from osteopathy.

Babies and toddlers: Cranial and paediatric osteopathy are often advised for babies and infants because of the gentle movements involved. However, all osteopaths are able to treat babies from the earliest days, and osteopathy is even used on premature babies. Once a baby has recovered from the initial shock of birth, an osteopath can deal with any head moulding necessary. This may be the case if medical intervention was used in the delivery, such as forceps or ventouse, or after a long second phase of labour, which subjects the baby's head to a lot of force. Osteopaths also treat colic, sleeplessness, reflux and glue ear, and work with babies who scream constantly and are distressed or fractious.

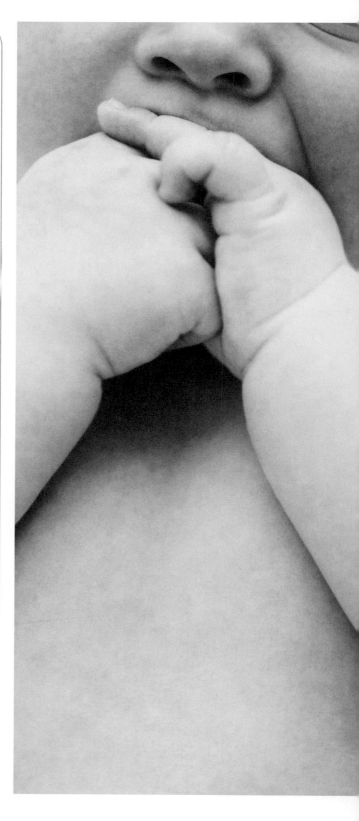

Homeopathy

Many parents turn to homeopathy as a natural treatment for common childhood illnesses, choosing homeopathic remedies, which are non-toxic, rather than conventional pharmaceutical drugs for their baby or child.

Homeopathy was founded by a German doctor, Samuel Hahnemann, in 1796. The basis of it is a belief that 'like may cure like' – similar to the medical theory underlying vaccination or immunization. Stimulating the body's own healing processes to cure the particular ailment or overpower the bacteria, rather than treating the symptoms themselves, is the idea. By introducing a remedy that mimics the symptoms, homeopathy builds the body's resistance.

Homeopaths emphasize that they treat people rather than diseases, and that a human being is more than the sum of his physical parts. Homeopathic medicine is said to be suitable for both acute and chronic conditions and is safe even for young children – a homeopath will prescribe remedies for babies suffering from problems such as colic.

Homeopathic remedies cannot cause side effects and you cannot become addicted to them. This is because only a very minute amount of the active ingredient is used in a specially prepared form. Many of the remedies are produced from herbs or plants, although conventional drugs can also be prescribed homeopathically, that is in very small amounts. Homeopaths believe the more dilute the concentration, the more powerful and effective it is. This is one of the aspects of homeopathy that many orthodox doctors find hard to accept.

What to Expect at a Consultation

In order to find the right remedy for you or your child, your homeopath needs to know all about you, so a detailed case study will be made. Finding out about general energy levels and past medical history is also important. This initial consultation may last an hour or more. Your homeopath will then prescribe a remedy, usually in tablet or powder form for adults, or as a

homeopathic treatment under the NHS

Ask your GP for a referral just as you would for any other hospital or specialist. Homeopathic treatment has been part of the NHS since the beginning and so you are entitled to treatment. Depending on where you live, you will be referred to a homeopathic hospital, a local NHS clinic or a local doctor with homeopathic training.
If your GP is resistant, explain your reasoning and stand your ground.

liquid for infants. Subsequent appointments usually last about half an hour.

The designation 6c or 30c after the name of a remedy refers to the degree of dilution. A remedy with a potency of 6c can be taken more frequently than one with a higher number.

If you are given homeopathic remedies to take at a later date, be sure to store them in a cool dark place, away from anything with a strong smell. If you are travelling, do not let the remedies go through an X-ray machine.

During treatment, your child may experience a period of exceptional well-being and optimism. Alternatively, she could get a cold, rash or some form of discharge that means her system is going through a cleaning stage. Sometimes symptoms can appear to get worse for a short time, which is usually a sign that the remedy is taking effect, but always check with the homeopathic practitioner.

In fact, if you or your child has any response to the treatment that concerns you, contact your homeopath straightaway. You may also want to make notes of any changes and take them with you to discuss at your next appointment.

Length of treatment depends on the individual. As a general rule, acute conditions respond more quickly, and the longer a chronic illness has existed, the longer it will take to disappear.

benefits of homeopathy

Pregnancy: Remedies are available to alleviate nausea and sickness, tiredness, cramps and heartburn, and to treat minor health problems associated with pregnancy, such as mild urinary problems, diarrhoea, anaemia, varicose veins, backache, thrush and emotional distress. Practitioners also say that homeopathy can be used to turn a breech baby, to deal with anxiety and fear and to tone the uterus, thus ensuring that the labour and birth go smoothly.

Labour: Homeopathic remedies can help produce strong effective contractions, stimulate the uterus if it fails, and deal with exhaustion and irritability.

Post-natal mothers: Remedies can aid fast recovery from damage to delicate tissues, and from exhaustion and bruising, and can help with baby blues and anxiety. Homeopathy can also help establish a good flow of milk for breast-feeding mothers and help protect the nipples from cracking and soreness. It is excellent for treating mastitis.

Babies and toddlers: A homeopath can treat babies suffering from colic, sleep problems, crying, teething, earache, nappy rash, fevers and chicken pox. For example, chamomilla, belladonna and pulsatilla can all be very effective during teething. The choice depends on the symptoms experienced. Babies tend to respond quickly to homeopathic treatment. The remedies are easy to administer and have no nasty taste.

WARNING Although over-the-counter remedies are available, you should never self-prescribe homeopathic medicines. In all cases, it is recommended that you contact a qualified homeopath for advice and treatment.

Medical Herbalism

The use of plants, or substances extracted from them, to try to cure illness is probably the oldest form of medicine known to man. Herbal medicine was practised in prehistoric times, and herbal treatments formed the basis of medical care in most ancient cultures, as they do among many people in developing countries around the world today.

As a parent, you may be drawn to herbalism as a non-toxic alternative to allopathic medicines. In fact, many drugs used by doctors today are derived from plants – for example, digoxin, which is used in the treatment of heart disease, is the synthesized form of digitalis from the foxglove.

Modern scientific interest in herbalism stems from a growing awareness that man-made drugs may have unpleasant, and sometimes serious, side effects. Many doctors accept the validity of herbalism and may refer patients on the NHS, particularly for chronic conditions. Meanwhile, extensive research is being carried out into the plant-based folk medicines of the native peoples of South America, Africa, China, Siberia and elsewhere.

Today, scientists find, extract and then synthesize in the laboratory a single active constituent from a plant – the part that has therapeutic value. That ingredient is manufactured on a large scale for use in pharmaceutical drugs. Herbal drugs, however, are extracts from sections of the whole plant – leaves, roots, berries – and contain hundreds, perhaps thousands, of plant constituents.

Herbalists believe that the active constituents are balanced within the plant and are made more, or less, powerful by the numerous other substances present. For example, synthetic diuretics seriously reduce the potassium level in the body, and this is restored using potassium supplements. The herbalist uses dandelion leaves, which are potent diuretics but also contain potassium to replace what is lost naturally.

Each culture has its herbal tradition, but Chinese herbal medicine is now proving to be very popular in the West. Traditional Chinese medicine works with about 10,000 different herbs. Western herbalists follow the same principles using different, indigenous plants. While Chinese herbs are especially popular for treatment of skin problems, practitioners can treat all physical conditions that don't require surgery or manipulation, and psychological problems as well. Many conditions are treated by a combination of herbs and acupuncture (see page 138) – the acupuncture relieves immediate symptoms, and the longer-term herbal treatment restores the balance of the body.

What to Expect at a Consultation

In Chinese medicine, diagnosis is made from looking at your tongue, taking the pulses in the wrists and observing your general appearance. Western medical herbalists are trained in the same diagnostic skills as orthodox doctors but take a more holistic approach to illness. The underlying cause of the problem is sought and, once diagnosed, treated, rather than the symptoms alone.

Herbal treatments may be prescribed in the form of a tincture (a weak, alcohol-based liquid), aqueous extracts, cream or compress, or a dried herb powder from which to make up a tea. This should be taken several times a day as prescribed. Treatment may include advice about diet and lifestyle as well as the herbal medicine.

benefits of medical herbalism

Pregnancy: Many of the usual complaints that crop up during pregnancy, such as morning sickness, constipation, headaches, tiredness and haemorrhoids, will respond to herbal treatment, when prescribed by a professional.

Labour: Increasingly, women are using herbs in the form of teas, tinctures or essential oils to facilitate a smooth labour. If you want to use herbs to influence contractions (hypertonic or stalled, for example), you should consult a practitioner. A professional, who can reliably liaise with other health professionals if necessary, will then be on hand throughout your care.

Post-natal mothers: You can use herbs after the birth of your baby for physical and emotional support. There are herbs to aid recovery from the impact of giving birth, to help heal wounds, to strengthen the system when the demands of breast-feeding hit you, and to soothe frazzled nerves when it all feels too much!

Useful herbs to enhance milk flow are raspberry, fennel and nettle. Herbs for lifting the spirits include lemon balm, lavender and St John's wort. Significant, prolonged post-natal depression should be treated by a qualified practitioner.

Babies and toddlers: Under the guidance of a qualified practitioner, medicinal plants and herbs can be used from a very early age to support your baby's general health or to treat specific problems. Depending on the age of your child, a herbalist may treat her via your breast milk or via aqueous extracts. Common complaints treated by herbalists include colic, sleep disorders, infections and digestive complaints.

greenfile

The most renowned herb associated with preparing for childbirth is raspberry leaf (*Rubus idaeus*). Available in a number of forms, the simplest way to take it is as a tea. Some women swear that it can bring on labour and make it easier, and even that it can help to restore the uterus to its non-pregnant state after the birth.

WARNING Although some plant-based treatments for minor ailments, particularly teas and infusions, are widely available and generally regarded as harmless, other plant derivatives are potentially dangerous. Therefore, it is recommended that you do not self-administer herbal treatments without the advice of a qualified and registered medical herbalist. Certain plants and herbs should be avoided during pregnancy and by infants, and anyone with a liver disease, such as hepatitis, or high blood pressure should consult their doctor before taking Chinese herbs.

Milestones

Newborn to Three Months

At birth, your baby's sight is rudimentary – she can focus at about 20–30cm and can study her mother's face as she breast-feeds – yet she has a limited perception of colour. She can distinguish high-pitched sounds better than low-pitched, and her hearing is especially attuned to the female human voice. As for recognition, your baby will know you by smell within hours, by voice within a day or two and by sight within a week. However, newborns can recognize something familiar for about 24 hours only. Take it away for an interval, and she won't remember it at all.

Your baby's progress is astounding. By six to twelve weeks, she's uncurled and is beginning to realize that her arms and legs belong to her. She looks at and listens to what's going on around her.

Three to Twelve Months

This is a delightful time for parents, with many 'firsts'. During these months your baby becomes a contributing member of the family, principally because she is now mobile and eats 'proper' food with the rest of the family.

Weaning marks a major transition for mother and baby – emotionally and physically. Most babies are ready to start solids when they are about four months old but it's important that you go at your baby's pace.

Getting about is the next hurdle for your developing baby. Her muscle control develops dramatically during this stage. By three months her neck and back muscles are strong enough for her to raise her head and chest. At four and a half months, she discovers that she can flip herself from her tummy onto her back. By around six months she can probably sit alone briefly and by eight months she's strong enough to sit unsupported. Now, her world changes dramatically. She can look around to see what's going on and pick up things that interest her.

After back control has developed, your baby will start to coordinate muscle control in her legs, which gives her the liberating ability to move from place to place. This is a major achievement but it also means that you'll have to be on your toes from now on, making sure the room is safe for an inquisitive, mobile baby.

The first stage of mobility is crawling. A few babies skip this stage altogether or substitute their own method of getting about, such as 'commando crawling' or 'walking like a bear', but, either way, it means she can reach what she wants rather than what you give her.

At the same time as your baby is mastering control of large body movements, she also learns to make finer movements. At first, she uses her whole hand, then she grasps things in a mitten-like grip, so she'll enjoy holding a biscuit and experimenting with feeding herself. By ten months, she has far greater control over each finger and can pick up small objects in a pincer grip.

Twelve to Eighteen Months

One of the most wondrous moments for parents is when their child takes her first steps. Most babies walk without support before they are fifteen months old but there is a great variation in starting ages. Once over this hurdle, the next is climbing and your baby will have an almost magnetic attraction to stairs. She will probably master going up quite quickly – but coming down is harder and it may take until she's about eighteen months to perfect.

By now, she is happily feeding herself, building towers out of blocks, fitting shapes into appropriate holes and generally refining her fine motor skills.

The other major milestone in this period is her speech development. During these six months she will start to understand and respond to simple instructions, such as 'wave bye-bye' and 'clap hands', and bring toys or objects from another room if asked. At her first birthday, she may speak one or two words besides 'mama' and 'dada' and by eighteen months, she'll speak forty to fifty words and even attempt two-word 'telegraphic' phrases, such as 'more juice' or 'daddy gone'. By now, you should be getting great delight from having a rudimentary dialogue with your child.

Two to Two and a Half Years

Language is the overriding theme of this stage of development. By her second birthday, your toddler will probably speak over two hundred words and understand as many as a thousand and she'll chatter away quite happily. She will talk in the here and now because the past and future hold no meaning for her. She will talk about herself as 'me' and ultimately 'I' but she may still refer to all men as 'dada' since children have a tendency to overgeneralize at first.

You will be driven mad by your toddler's capacity to ask endless questions of the 'why' and 'what' variety, but it is symptomatic of her increasing awareness of herself as an individual. This drive for autonomy also leads to the frustrating 'me do it' phase, which often leads to conflicts between parents and child.

Two and a Half to Three Years

Better coordination and balance and stronger legs open up a whole new world of adventure for this age group. They can now learn to pedal tricycles properly, to run, climb and even to jump. A first attempt at throwing and catching will probably be made at around this age.

By now, your chattering toddler will probably be understood by strangers and her charming, idiosyncratic pronunciations of certain words are starting to be ironed out. It's almost impossible to put a number on her vocabulary but she is well able to sustain a rewarding conversation with you and others.

Your child will now be playing with other children, and she and her playmates will learn new skills from one another. They often come up with creative ideas together, or solve a problem, or even learn new words that they haven't used before. Although the notion of sharing comes slowly to most toddlers and a good deal of their play ends in squabbles over possession, this in itself can teach them valuable lessons about bargaining and negotiating – if you can stand not to intervene, that is.

Eighteen Months to Two Years

As her balance improves, so the eighteen-month-old becomes more confident at walking and turning, and she may enjoy riding a push-along toy. Many children are riding a tricycle by two, but probably still pushing it along with their feet.

Her fine motor skills have also improved considerably, and she is now able to make a tower of three bricks, post shapes and stack with aplomb. She will also love the feel of brush or pencil on paper and will be fascinated by the fact that she can make her own mark.

By now, your toddler probably has a vocabulary of about fifty words and understands perhaps four times that many, and she'll be using these words with great relish while adding to them daily.

Milestones Summary Chart

	Birth–3 months	3–6 months	6–12 months	1–2 years	2–3 years
MOBILITY	Lifts head while lying on front	Rolls over	Sits without support Trying to crawl Stands holding onto furniture	Stands alone Walking Climbing stairs Kicks or throws a ball	Pedals a tricycle Runs and jumps
COORDINATION	Grasp reflex	Holds a rattle Reaches out for objects	Uses mitten grip, then pincer grip to hold objects Uses either hand and can drop items from ten months	Uses a spoon and holds a cup Shape sorting Feeding self Building towers of blocks	Scribbles with crayon or pencils Paints
SPEECH	Cooing	Imitates sounds	Babbles Squeals with delight Shouts for attention Uses pitch	Starts with three or four words By 18 months has around 40–50 words Uses two-word 'telegraphic' phrases Refers to herself by name Tries to sing	Talks well in sentences, chants rhymes and songs
SOCIAL SKILLS	Smiling at familiar faces Listens to speech	Changes expression when displeased Distinguishes people Attachment formed to a chosen person Laughs	Wariness of strangers Uses gestures to indicate Points Babbling	First conversations Understands and responds Plays independently but in parallel	Plays with other children
PHYSICAL CHANGES	Cooing Hands open Colour vision develops	Uncurled	First teeth appear	Left- or right-handedness established All 20 primary teeth through	Head more in proportion to body

Useful Contacts

Nurture and Care

FSID (Foundation for the Study of Infant Deaths)
www.fsid.org.uk
Advice and support for those affected by cot death.
Helpline: 020 7233 2090

Maternity Action
www.maternityaction.org.uk
Advice to pregnant women and new parents.

La Leche League GB
www.laleche.org.uk
Breast-feeding information and support.
Helpline: 0845 120 2918

National Childbirth Trust (NCT)
www.nct.org.uk
Support for parents during pregnancy, birth and early days of parenthood.
Pregnancy and birth helpline:
0300 33 00 772
Breast-feeding helpline: 0300 33 00 771
Enquiries: 0300 33 00 770

NHS Direct
www.nhsdirect.nhs.uk
Health advice and information.
Helpline: 0845 4647

Healthy Home Environment

Rugmark
www.rugmark.org
Charity working to end child labour in the carpet industry in South Asia.

RoSPA
www.childcarseats.org.uk
Details of UK legislation on child car seats.

Department of Transport
www.thinkroadsafety.gov.uk
Details of UK legislation on child car seats.

National Society for the Prevention of Cruelty to Children
www.nspcc.org.uk
Offers counselling and advice to parents.

Natural Learning

International Association for Steiner/Waldorf Early Childhood Education
www.iaswece.org
Information on Steiner/Waldorf kindergartens and schools.

Steiner Waldorf Schools Fellowship
www.steinerwaldorf.org
Information on Steiner education in UK and Ireland.

Montessori Schools UK
www.montessori.org.uk
The main national database for Montessori nursery and junior schools.

International Montessori
www.montessori.edu
The official international Montessori site with links to schools and organizations.

AMI (Association Montessori International)
www.montessori-ami.org

Education Otherwise
www.education-otherwise.org
Takes its name from the law that states: 'either by regular attendance at school or otherwise.'

Home Education Special
www.he-special.org.uk
For parents who are interested in home educating a child with special educational needs.

Home Education Advisory Service
www.heas.org.uk
Help with home schooling in the UK.

Home Education
www.home-education.org.uk
Home-schooling information, including UK laws concerning compulsory education.

UK Government Home Education Guidelines
www.dcsf.gov.uk/localauthorities/index.cfm
Government and local authority guidelines for home education.

Home Education & Family Services (HEFS)
www.homeeducator.com/HEFS/index.htm
Advice for home-educators across the USA and the rest of world.

Health and Healing

CRY-SIS
www.cry-sis.org.uk
Support for parents of crying, screaming and sleepless babies.

Home Start UK
www.home-start.org.uk
UK family support.

Toilet Training
This subject troubles many parents. It certainly needs to be attempted at the right time and with the right mental approach. Experts and parents alike have a lot to say on the subject – certainly more than we can cover comfortably here – but there are some good websites that you might like to consult. Try visiting:

www.babycentre.co.uk/toddler/pottytraining

www.safekids.co.uk/PottyTraining.html

www.askbaby.com/potty-training.htm

Natural Therapies

Complementary Medical Association
www.the-cma.org.uk
For information on complementary therapies and lists of local practitioners.

British Acupuncture Council
www.acupuncture.org.uk
The UK's main regulatory body for the practice of traditional acupuncture by more than 2,800 acupuncturists.

The General Chiropractic Council
www.gcc-uk.org
The regulatory body for chiropractors in the UK.

General Council for Massage Therapies
www.gcmt.org.uk
The governing body for massage therapies and all bodyworks and soft tissue techniques in the UK.

General Osteopathic Council
www.osteopathy.org.uk
Provides a register of qualified osteopaths for the UK.

The Foundation for Paediatric Osteopathy
www.fpo.org.uk
Information and advice on osteopathy for babies and children.

The Society of Homeopaths
www.homeopathy-soh.org
Online searchable register of qualified practitioners, articles and list of UK accredited schools.

British Homeopathic Association
www.trusthomeopathy.org
Information plus lists relevant doctors in the UK.

The Homeopathic Medical Association
www.the-hma.org
Lists registered practitioners in UK.

National Institute of Medical Herbalists
www.nimh.org.uk
The UK's leading professional body representing herbal practitioners.

Index

actions, louder than
    words 87–8, 89
activities,
    bad-weather 111
    organized 111
    physical 110–11
acupressure 138–9
acupuncture 138, 139
air quality 42, 58
allergens, in old carpets 45
art, creative 108
asthma 60
audio books 106

baby foods 21
backpacks 50
bathing,
    for chicken pox 128
    newborns 65
bedtime rituals 37
bites,
    human 130
    insect 130
blisters 128, 133
body language 87–9
bonding 10–13
    delayed 12–13
    helping the process 13
bottle feeding 17, 18
breast feeding 15,
    16–17, 18
    expressing milk 16
bruises 132

car seats 50
carpets 45
carriers 50
chemicals 57
    in cloth production 46
    dry-cleaning 54
    gardens 61
    in paint 44
chicken broth 126
chicken pox 128

childcare,
    choosing 75
    early provision 72–6
childminders 72
chiropractic 140–1
choking 33, 127
chopping boards 52
cleaning products 7,
    52–3, 57
clothing 63
colds 127
colic 114, 116
    chiropractic for 140
    massage for 114, 142
communication 87–9, 154
convulsions, febrile
    (fits) 124
cots 49
cotton, organically
    grown 46
coughs 126, 127
cradle cap 118
crayons 108
crying,
    obvious causes 116
    and parental stress 116
cultural heritage 104
cuts and scrapes 132

dance 93–4
day nurseries 72, 75
daytime sleep 38–9
dental care 23
detergents 54
diarrhoea 121
discipline 87–8
disinfectants 53
disposable nappies 117
drawing 108
dressing up 103
dry-cleaning 54
dummy,
    for colic 114
    to settle for sleep 39
dust mites 45, 46

ear infection 123
eating habits, good 27–8
electromagnetic fields 58
emotional intelligence
    81–4
    ability test 82
empathy,
    innate 84
    tuning in to your
        child 89
exercise 110–11

fairy tales 104, 106, 107
fantasy play 96, 98
feeding milestones 33
fevers 124
    at teething 24
first aid 132–3
fontanelles 118
food,
    early 27–33
    good eating habits 27–8
food intolerance 31
fruit 29–30
    home-grown 28
    puréed 20, 21
furniture 49–50

gardens, chemicals 61
Goleman, Daniel 82

Hahnemann, Samuel 148
hand-knits 63
health 113–35
    baby 114–18
    common complaints
        121–4
    natural 7
    passive smoking risk 60
heating 58
herbal teas 116, 121,
    127, 129
herbalism, medical 150–1
home schooling 78–9

homeopathic remedies
    118, 123
    for colds 127
    first aid 132–3
    insect bites 130
homeopathy 148–9
    benefits 149
    NHS treatment 148
honey 30, 128, 132
hygiene 57

imitation 98
immune system 126–9
impulse-control 82
insect bites 130
IQ ratings 81

kindergarten 76

labour,
    acupressure in 139
    chiropractic 140–1
    herbalism 151
    homeopathy in 149
    massage in 145
lactose intolerance 31
laser acupuncture 139
lead, in old paint 43–4
learning,
    helping your child 71
    natural 67–71
    positive environment
        for 68, 70

make-believe tales 106–7
manuka honey 128, 132
mask, to make 103
massage 12, 114, 142–5
    benefits of 145
    for premature babies
        142
    relaxing 144
materials, for play and
    learning 68, 70
medical herbalism 150–1

medicine, for fevers 124
milestones 152–3, 154
    feeding 33
mistakes, learning from 71
modelling dough,
    home-made 70
Montessori system 76
moods 85
moral sense, from
    story-telling 107
motion sickness 135
mould and mildew 53
movement,
    development of 154
    as language 92
mumps 129
music 92, 94–5
musical talent 94

nannies 72
nappies and nappy rash
    117–18
National Childbirth Trust
    13
natural fabrics,
    for clothes 63
    flooring 45
    soft furnishings and
    bedding 45–6
    wall coverings 44
natural medicine 112,
    126, 128
natural products,
    baby equipment 49–50
    for cleaning 52–4, 57
    in paints 44
    in toiletries 6
natural remedies,
    breast feeding problems
    16
    for coughs and colds
    126, 127
    lavender oil to aid sleep
    37
    for nappy rash 118
    teething 24
natural therapies 137–51

nose, blowing 123
nursery,
    bedding and soft
    furnishings 45–6
    ecology of 42–6
    furniture 49–50
nursery schools 76

obesity 7, 109
organic food 6
    baby foods 21
osteopathy 146–7

paints,
    natural 44
    for nursery 43–4
    for play 108
Palmer, Daniel David 140
Piaget, Jean 99
play and creativity 91–111
    creative art 108
    creative play 96–9
    imaginary play 100–3
    music and movement
    92–5
    storytelling 104–7
playgroups 75
pollutants 57–61
    combustion 58
post-natal depression 12
post-natal mothers,
    acupressure for 139
    chiropractic 141
    herbalism 151
    homeopathy for 149
    lack of sleep 15–16, 34
    massage for 145
    osteopathy for 147
potato prints 109
prams 50
pregnancy,
    acupressure in 139
    chiropractic 141
    herbalism 151
    homeopathy in 149
    massage in 145
    osteopathy in 147

pressure to conform 68
probiotics 118, 121, 123
puréed foods 20, 21

radon poisoning 60
reading stories 107
respiratory disease 60
Rugmark, for carpets 45

safety precautions
    49–50, 55
    and standards 50
saline nose drops 127
Salovey, Peter and Mayer,
    John 82
salt, limiting 30–1
schooling 71
    home 78–9
    special needs 79
shaker rattle, home-made
    95
singing 94–5
sleep 34–9
    bedtime rituals 37
    daytime 38–9
    and early waking 39
    and leaving baby to cry
    37–8
    mother's lack of
    15–16, 34
    moving to own bed 38
    and night-time feeds
    34, 36
slug traps 61
smoking, passive 60–1
snacks and treats 31
socialization 75, 76,
    79, 154
sodium see salt
splints 133
spontaneity 100
sprains and strains 133
Steiner, Rudolf 75, 104
storage, nursery 49–50
strollers 50
Sudden Infant Death
    Syndrome (SIDS) 39, 60
sugar 30

teething 23–4
    toys 24
temperature, taking 124
terry cotton nappies 117
time,
    for meals 28
    and space 98–9
toddler groups 75
toiletries 65
toxic fumes,
    in carpets 45
    in paint 44
toys,
    home-made 100
    props for imaginary
    play 103
traditional Chinese
    medicine 138, 150

vaccination 129
vegetables 29–30
    home-grown 28
    puréed 20, 21
vitamins,
    deficiencies 132
    fruit and vegetables
    28, 30

wallpapers, for nursery 44
washing products 54
water 21, 121, 128
weaning, first solid foods
    20–1
working parents 77

Acknowledgements

I would like to thank Liz Dean, my editor, for taking so much care in the production of this book and for making it such a delight to work on. Also, my thanks to Chelsey Fox, my friend and agent, for putting Cindy at CICO Books and myself in touch.

Finally, I would like to thank my husband, Nick, for his continued and unwavering support and my two sons, Alex and George, on whom I cut my natural parenting teeth, and who have grown from delightful babies into glorious boys.

Picture Credits

Key: a=above, b=below, r=right, l=left, c=centre.

Caroline Arber
page 100
Vanessa Davies
pages 1, 3, 5cb, 5b, 7, 43, 44, 45, 46r, 63, 64, 73, 76, 88, 90, 95, 98, 112, 114, 116, 119, 125, 127, 128, 134, 139, 140, 143, 146, 153, 155
Christopher Drake
pages 6, 51, 54, 66, 97
Dan Duchars
pages 8, 11, 14, 25, 40, 80, 86, 105, 144 all, 145
Tara Fisher
pages 21, 27, 33 both
Richard Jung
page 28b
William Lingwood
page 52
Emma Mitchell
page 131
Daniel Pangbourne
pages 5ac, 10, 12, 22, 24a, 26, 29, 36, 56, 59, 70, 71, 77, 78, 81, 83, 85, 87, 102, 104, 106, 110, 111
Debbie Patterson
page 109
© Photolibrary
pages 93, 94

William Reavell
page 28a
Claire Richardson
page 62
© Stockbyte
pages 2, 5bcb, 84, 89, 115, 122, 136, 138, 141, 147, 149
Lucinda Symons
page 55
Debi Treloar
pages 5a, 13, 15, 19, 20, 32, 35, 37, 38, 47, 74, 117, 120, 129
Polly Wreford
pages 5aca, 17, 46l, 48, 69, 96, 99, 101
Francesca Yorke
page 30

Front cover: Freya by Vanessa Davies
Jacket spine: Florence by Debi Treloar
Back cover (clockwise from top left): Charlie by Tara Fisher; Rebecca and Ruben by Dan Duchars; Emilia by Tara Fisher.

Special thanks to our models Trisha and Aoife; Kate and Freya; and Tola and Luca.